WAYNE BARKER

Bernard O'Mahoney is the bestselling author of *Essex Boys*, *Essex Boys: The New Generation*, *Bonded by Blood* and numerous other acclaimed true-crime titles.

WAYNE BARKER
Born to Fight

BERNARD O'MAHONEY

MAINSTREAM
PUBLISHING

EDINBURGH AND LONDON

I dedicate this book to my children,

JAMES, HENRY, WAYNE, CHARLOTTE, KANE AND BENJAMIN.

Acknowledgements

I WISH TO thank Wayne's sister Lorraine for the help she gave me in completing this book. Also Wayne's partner Claire for being so humble. David Fraser, I thank you for being so compassionate about your friend. Wayne thought the world of you.

A huge thank you to my beautiful wife, Roshea, to Paddy the Laddy, Adrian, Vinney, Karis, Daine and Lydia, as well as to my grandson Charlie-Joe. I look forward to welcoming into the world my granddaughter Poppy, courtesy of Karis and Paul, and twins Alannah and Micky courtesy of Vinney and Hayley. The only wealth in this world, as Wayne discovered, is our children. Treat them well – because they get to choose your retirement home!

Bernard O'Mahoney

Contents

Preface

MY PLAN FOR the future is to stay alive as long as I can and beat this cancer. We all share the same destination and every man that has ever lived has tried to avoid arriving there. I have accepted I must die, but I refuse to accept that it will be cancer that will kill me. To concede that would be like throwing in the towel midway through a fight and that won't ever happen in my life. I have to focus on the fight ahead and ensure that my family are looked after.

I am 52 years old as I write this; I have at least another 23 years of my life to live. Here's hoping that any of my future addresses are not preceded by the letters HMP, my health improves and all those I have wronged in my life can forgive me.

Wayne Barker, January 2012

Ladies and Gentlemen, Mr Wayne Barker

10.42 A.M., 21 December 2011. I have received some distressing phone calls in my life but few have alarmed or moved me in the way Wayne Barker's did this morning. 'They have given me six months to live, Bernie, but I am not having it. I have found a surgeon in London who will operate on me tomorrow. It's going to cost me a lot of money, but if it's successful I get a little while longer to live. If it goes wrong, I will probably die on the operating table. There are no guarantees, so if I do die I just want you to know that it's been a pleasure knowing you.'

How do you respond to such a statement? What do you say to someone knowing it may be your last-ever conversation? As Wayne himself would say, 'My head fell off.'

'Don't say that Wayne,' I eventually managed to reply. 'You've been on the canvas before and got back up fighting. Let's not say goodbye. Let's just say that we will meet up when you get out of hospital.'

'That will do, Bernie. I shall see you soon. Take care and make sure you finish my book,' Wayne said before hanging up the phone.

Unsurprisingly, Wayne emerged from the operating

theatre ready for the next round in what became the hardest fight of his life. That is what Wayne Barker was all about: never backing down and never giving up, regardless of the opposition. I am not implying that he was some Terminator figure who couldn't be beaten – like any honest man, Wayne would admit that he had tasted defeat – but it was his spirit that I personally found unique and admirable.

I first met Wayne Barker while working on a book titled *Faces*. His name continually cropped up during interviews with some of the most notorious villains in the UK. 'You must include Wayne Barker,' Mad Frankie Fraser had said. 'He is a man's man, the real deal, a true face.'

Arriving at Wayne's Manchester home one morning some weeks later, I felt as if I were walking onto the set of a *Godfather* movie. At the head of a large boardroom table sat Wayne and all around him were villains from Manchester, Bradford and Leeds, who listened intently as he addressed the smoke-filled room. No sentence was completed without his phone ringing; Nick from Manchester, David in London and Ryan in Leeds all had problems that Wayne told them he could resolve. 'Fuck him. He's a fool. Tell him to come to my house in the morning or he'll lose a lot more than he owes if he doesn't pay' was one of the pearls of wisdom that was passed to a caller. As well as the insistent phone calls, every 30 minutes or so somebody would knock on Wayne's front door and either a wad of money would be handed over or a group of men would be hustled into the kitchen, where Wayne would tell them in no uncertain terms what was going to happen next.

I instantly liked Wayne and after talking to him at length thought that his life story would make a fascinating book. In the past, Wayne had been approached by a journalist who wanted to write his story, but he had felt it was too early in his life to do so. By the time I met Wayne, he had been diagnosed with cancer and he felt it would be at least worth recording his story on tape. However, he insisted that it was simply a precautionary measure and not an admission that he was preparing to die – not just yet.

Over the weeks and months that followed, I spent many hours with Wayne as he told me all about his unorthodox upbringing and remarkable adventures in life. From Salford to St Louis, Missouri, Wayne Barker has left a lasting impression on every man and woman he has ever met. I have tried hard to categorise Wayne; con man, wise man, fighter, thief? He fits none yet all of those descriptions, because he is simply so much more. That statement may not make sense to you now, but after reading a few chapters about this gentleman's life it will dawn on you that it makes perfect sense. So, without further ado, ladies and gentlemen, it is my pleasure to introduce to you Mr Wayne Barker . . .

Bernard O'Mahoney

ROUND ONE

Stairway to Heaven

I WAS BORN on Sunday, 29 November 1959. That very same day the Reverend Martin Luther King, Jr., preached his final sermon as pastor of the Dexter Avenue Baptist Church in Montgomery, Alabama, after resigning to devote more time to the civil-rights movement. Rahm Emanuel, the former White House chief of staff and current mayor of Chicago, Illinois, was also born that day. It's interesting that Martin Luther King, who represented oppressed people, and Rahm Emanuel, who represents a city synonymous with gangsters, should both be linked with the day I was born. I say that because I am a man who, not unlike the Reverend King, has always backed those perceived to be the underdog, and, like Rahm Emanuel's city, my day-to-day activities have often involved people whom society has deemed to be gangsters or villains.

My youth was like an Open University course in criminality, with practical tutorials in many of its fine arts, such as fraud and deception. But after considering the many diverse aspects of crime, I was only ever going to major in one: the profession of violence. It has been a part of my life for as long as I can recall, and when my time comes I hope I am strong enough in mind and body to leave this particular stage the only way I know how: fighting.

WAYNE BARKER

My grandfather, 'Potty' Barker, was well known in Manchester during the '50s and '60s. He frequented the pubs and clubs where the city's most notorious villains socialised. He was known as 'Potty' because he was from Stoke-on-Trent in Staffordshire, which is known as 'the Potteries'. It is so called because the town is considered to be the home of the pottery industry in England. My grandfather had a soft spot for me. He would take me out with him while he was conducting his business, and he taught me how to earn money, deal with situations and, of course, conduct myself in the company of others.

When I was about 15 years old, my grandfather and I went into the Long Bar in Piccadilly, a busy pub near Manchester railway station that was very popular with the criminal fraternity. As we entered, my grandfather noticed a mixed-race man named George King standing at the bar and made his way across the room to speak to him. My grandfather and George were good friends going back many years. George was an ex-boxer who had a car pitch on Chorlton Road. I wouldn't describe him as a villain, but he used to wheel and deal in cars and contraband, and he had a reputation as a hard man based on his forthright attitude and boxing skills. George was an imposing figure; he was in his mid-50s at this time, a big, thickset man, always dressed immaculately in a suit and full-length Crombie coat. He shook my hand and put a ten-shilling note in my pocket. It was customary for villains to give the young and old money if they were in their company back in those days. I knew I shouldn't stand, mouth agape, listening while men spoke, so I found a seat for myself and my grandfather and sat down.

When my grandfather had finished talking to George a few minutes later, he bought us both a drink and joined me. Shortly afterwards, a man in his early 20s named Brian Dolan entered the bar. He walked straight up to George King and punched him. George hit the ground like he had been shot. Dolan, or 'Crazy Horse' as he was also known, stood over George and said, 'Stay down, old man, because if you get up I will write you off.' He then picked up George's pint, drank it in one go and walked out of the pub. Everybody in the bar continued to chat and drink as if nothing had happened.

As my grandfather drove me home, he said to me, 'What happened to George is known as Gunfighter Syndrome.' I didn't have a clue what my grandfather was talking about, so I asked him to explain. He replied, 'It's when a young pup comes up against an old dog. Everyone gets old, son. You just have to know when you're past your best and accept that fact.'

Those wise words have stuck with me all of my life. So much so, I was planning for my retirement long before I had grown into an adult. I decided that when I reached 50 I would throw in the towel and retire to enjoy whatever was left of my life in peace.

Everything went pretty much according to plan until just before I reached my 50th birthday. I can't stand by and watch people do things in a way that doesn't meet with my approval. I like things done right. My home, my clothes, even the way I eat and drink, have to be just so. It's the way I was brought up and it's the way I shall die. It's that meticulous attitude to life and the orderly way in which I conduct myself that saw me clambering up a 16-ft stepladder above the stage of my nightclub in Droylsden, Manchester. I had sat and watched a young guy messing about trying to adjust the stage lighting rig for what seemed an eternity. That evening an all-girl band were due to perform at a function and I wanted everything ready before they arrived. The way the guy was tinkering about the band would have retired, never mind arrived to perform, before he had finished. My club – the

Manchester Prize Fighters' Club – had a reputation for efficiency and good service, and it was a status that I wished to uphold. When I watch 'messers', I just get more and more irate until I either intervene and do the job myself or explode into a rage. I rarely do the latter, so I said to the lad, 'Get down the ladder. We haven't got all day. I will do it.'

A few weeks earlier I had undergone minor surgery for a repetitive strain injury to my right arm. I had fought on the cobbles and in the ring throughout my entire life and the constant pressure from pounding heads, bodies and punchbags had taken its toll on my joints. As a result of the operation, my right arm was in a sling, which made climbing the stepladder a little more hazardous. Even more testing was that having arrived at the top of the steps I then had to let go with my left arm in order to adjust the lighting rig. Cursing the young man's inefficiency, I pushed and pulled the rig until it was finally where I wanted it to be and then I began to descend the steps. With the benefit of hindsight, I suppose it was inevitable: I somehow lost my footing and fell. The full impact caught me just under the ribs. I have taken some powerful body shots in my life, but this felt like I had been hit by a freight train.

People ran to my aid, but I leapt to my feet and told them to keep back. 'I'm all right, I'm all right,' I lied. I couldn't breathe and I instinctively knew that my ribs had been broken. I have suffered more broken ribs than I care to remember while fighting. Damage of this nature caused to a fighter is usually to the left or right side of the ribcage, but this injury was at the front. The pain was extreme, but there's nothing one can really do to treat broken ribs other than grin and bear it until they heal. So I didn't bother seeking medical attention. I just strapped my chest with bandages, grimaced and got on with taking care of business.

A few weeks before my 50th birthday, I began to suffer

with chronic indigestion and ended up drinking Gaviscon, a medication for heartburn and indigestion, by the bottle. I assumed that my broken ribs had trapped something inside me that was causing my body to produce excess bile or acid, so I went to my GP, Dr John Danson, for advice. As I am financially secure, I refuse to burden the NHS with any health problems that I have and so I pay for private health care. I have total faith in Dr Danson. He is no ordinary GP. The care and dedication he shows each and every one of his patients, private or otherwise, is second to none. I admire him as a man and a professional immensely and am proud that he considers me to be a friend. Dr Danson carried out a few tests and then sent me for an ultrasound scan at the Highfield Hospital in Rochdale. My chest and abdomen were smeared with some sort of jelly and the staff then used a machine that produced sound waves to create images of organs and structures inside the body. Fortunately, they couldn't detect anything of concern and I was allowed to return home the same day.

We all know our own bodies. A sixth sense tells us when something isn't right, and I just knew that despite the results of the scan something in my chest or stomach needed attention. I mentioned this to Dr Danson, so, to be on the safe side, he sent me to the Spire Hospital in Whalley Range, Manchester, for a colonoscopy. It is a pain-free procedure that involves a fibre optic camera being inserted into the anus so that the large bowel and distal part of the small bowel (the final two feet of the colon) can be checked for diseases such as cancer. The procedure might not have caused pain, but it certainly made up for that by creating embarrassment. I genuinely didn't know where to look as the hospital staff went about their work. I was pleased when it was over and even more pleased when I was informed that nothing of significance had been found.

The only problem was that my physical condition had not changed. I wasn't bedridden or unable to leave my home – on the contrary I attended numerous parties over Christmas and New Year – but I still had to drink Gaviscon by the bottle to prevent me from being sick or suffering horrendous indigestion. I returned to Dr Danson and explained that my condition was not improving. He assured me that the tests had indicated that I was fit and healthy, but I just knew something was not quite right and told him so. To allay my fears and be 100 per cent sure that I was well, Dr Danson picked up the telephone and booked me into the Spire Hospital for an endoscopy on Monday, 8 February 2010. An endoscope is a flexible telescope about the thickness of a little finger. The endoscope is passed through the mouth, into the oesophagus and down towards the stomach. A small camera at the end of the endoscope allows medical staff to check for diseases or other health issues. I don't mind admitting I was terrified and my courage had completely diminished. I wasn't concerned about any possible outcome; I just did not fancy having anything shoved down my throat that I wasn't in control of.

Two days before my appointment was due to take place, there was to be a wedding reception at my club. Prior to going into work that morning I had visited the Café Rouge on Deansgate in Manchester to meet a few friends. I can be found there most mornings having breakfast. I am a creature of habit. I always order eggs Hemingway (poached eggs and salmon) and have usually left by 11.30 a.m. When I arrived at my club just before lunchtime that day, I was my usual self, ordering the staff to get their act together and chasing people up so that everything would be perfect for the happy couple's reception that night. By late afternoon, everything was in place and so I sent the staff home to freshen up and get changed in preparation for the evening. I am very old school. I insist upon the staff wearing bow ties, greeting guests with a smile, champagne – and courtesy, of course, is paramount. Three hundred guests attended the event and it was a real success.

Towards the end of the night, I was in my office checking the takings and doing a bit of necessary paperwork. I felt hungry, so I telephoned a Chinese restaurant in Ashton-under-Lyne that I used regularly and ordered some food. By the time the food had arrived, the guests had all gone home, so some of the staff joined me in the office to eat. I had a bit of duck and chicken chow mein, but for some reason it didn't taste right to me. I asked the staff if they thought the food was off, but they all said it was delicious. Sitting at the table, I began to feel nauseated, so I asked somebody to fetch me a drink. 'That's ropey, that food. It's given me food poisoning,' I said. The staff were adamant that the food tasted fine, so I just sat in silence watching them eat. I began to feel increasingly unwell, and when they had finished eating I told them to go home and return the following day to clean up. This news was met with whoops of joy, because normal practice after an event is for everybody to stay behind, clean up, stock the bar and then head home at four or five in the morning. When the staff had left, I drove straight home and got into bed, hoping that by the time I woke up my stomach would have settled.

At approximately 8.30 a.m., I awoke to find that I looked like an expectant mother. My stomach was three times its normal size and felt like a lump of rock. As quickly as possible, I made my way to the bathroom, where I began to be violently sick. I drank a glass of water, but the moment it touched my stomach I threw it back up. My wife, Sharon, must have heard me vomiting because she ran to my aid and asked if everything was OK. I explained that I had eaten a Chinese takeaway that had tasted off and reassured her that I would be fine. I asked my wife to fetch me another pint of water, but when I drank it I was sick. I did this five or six times, thinking that I was flushing out any contaminated food from my stomach. I was really sweating, and thinking, 'I have never had food poisoning as bad as this.' When I drank the next pint of water, the eggs Hemingway that I had eaten for breakfast the previous day came up totally undigested. As soon as I saw the food bobbing about in the toilet, I said to my wife, 'Phone me an ambulance now. I'm in trouble.' My breakfast had been in my stomach for approximately 30 hours and had not been digested, so I knew something serious was wrong.

A few minutes later, the ambulance arrived and I was whisked away to the Royal Oldham Hospital, where I was given morphine to ease the extreme pain that I was experiencing. I was X-rayed and then put into a private room, where I remained for two days. I had no idea what was going on around me because of the effects of the morphine.

I do recall that a surgeon named Dr Rate came in to see me. He seemed very abrupt, which annoyed me at the time. He said that the X-rays did not show any kind of problem and so they were going to carry out an exploratory operation. I formed the impression that Dr Rate was insinuating that there was nothing wrong with me and I was somehow overreacting to a little food poisoning. It's fair to say that the atmosphere my mood created between Dr Rate and me wasn't great.

The following morning, I was awoken around seven, washed and then wheeled down to an operating theatre on a trolley. I can recall that there were two other patients awaiting surgery. An elderly lady to my left was having something done to her hip and a man to my right was having his shoulder sorted out. I felt relaxed, happy almost. As far as I was concerned, a surgeon was going to open me up and sort out whatever it was that had been giving me a bad stomach.

When I did eventually awake, I was on a ward and the curtains were drawn around me. I don't know the medical term for my condition, but I self-diagnosed that I was off my fucking trolley because of the morphine that had and was still being pumped into me. As I slowly began to focus, I could see that three doctors were standing at the foot of my bed. 'Mr Barker? Mr Barker, can you hear me?' one of them said. When I eventually acknowledged the doctor, he explained that they had removed two tumours from my colon, one of which had been perforated. 'You are very fortunate to have survived, Mr Barker, very fortunate,' the doctor said.

At that time, I genuinely believed that I was one of the fittest men on the planet. I had trained hard and fought all of my life, yet here was a doctor telling me that I was lucky to be alive. I was, to say the least, extremely shocked. 'Tumours? What kind of tumours?' I enquired. Before turning and walking away, one of the doctors nonchalantly replied, 'Cancerous tumours, Mr Barker.'

I don't know how long I lay in bed staring into space, but it was some time before I was able to pick up a telephone and call my wife. I cannot tell you when I had last cried before that day, but at that moment I couldn't help myself. I considered crying a weakness, so my reaction shocked not only me but my wife, too. She knew something was seriously wrong when I broke down, so she demanded to know what it was, but I could only say, 'I've got cancer,' before hanging up the phone.

Thirty minutes later, my wife was at my bedside, and I did my best to explain to her all that had happened and what I had been told. I was in a morphine-created haze and confused, so it's unlikely that I made much sense. I can remember us holding each other and sobbing, but little else. I cannot even recall my wife leaving.

25

I have vague memories of friends being at my bedside at different stages of that evening, but what was said I really cannot recall. At around midnight, a very dear friend of mine named Julie Perry came to see me, having flown in from New York. It was an emotional meeting. Julie gave me a set of rosary beads that had been blessed by the Pope and sat next to me for several hours talking about old times. Little of it registered; her voice was like a pleasant background noise. I was in emotional turmoil and unable to say much, but I was comforted by the simple fact that she was there.

When Julie finally left and I was alone, I was engulfed by feelings of immense anger. How could this happen to me? Why was this happening to me? Wayne Barker had too much to live for. I summoned the hospital staff and told them that I wanted moving off the ward and into a private room, that I needed to be alone. My request was denied, so the following morning I asked to be taken from the hospital to a private facility. On reflection, I should not have been so abrasive and abrupt towards the hospital staff, but I was understandably upset. Thankfully they understood that I was in shock and distressed. After the doctors had completed their rounds, I was taken by private ambulance to the Highfield Hospital in Rochdale. I was put in a private room and left alone with my thoughts.

I don't mind admitting that I was absolutely terrified as I relived the events of the previous two days. How many more days would I get to spend with my loved ones? Was it years, months or days before I would die? I panicked and began ringing people to sell personal items such as my car and jewellery. I called in debts and tied up as many loose business ends as possible. As it was a private hospital, family and friends could visit 24 hours a day, every day. Soon my room resembled a busy office as car dealers, con men, crooks and businessmen arrived to buy, sell or sort out ongoing matters with me. The noise we made as we sought agreement soon attracted complaints from other patients and their families, so a doctor was dispatched to speak to me.

My first encounter with Dr Rate at the Royal Oldham had not been very pleasant, so I prepared myself for an acrimonious exchange when I saw that it was him striding towards my bed.

'You're too loud, Mr Barker, and you're having too many visitors,' he said when he reached me.

'Who the fuck are you, mate? Who are you? I pay for private health care. I am a popular person and a lot of people depend on me. I cannot afford to fucking die. What is your problem regarding my visitors?' I shouted.

Dr Rate did not answer; he just turned and walked away. Two days later, he came to see me and we resolved our differences amicably. We have since become good friends.

Ten days after being admitted to the Highfield Hospital I was discharged weighing just 10½ stone. I had 18 staples in my stomach and £90,000 in a bag (the proceeds of selling some of my personal possessions). As I climbed into my wife's car, I could feel the red mist descending. I wasn't ready to fucking die. How and why had this terrible disease invaded my body? The first person I rang owed me only ten pounds, but I still managed to shout, scream and threaten him with violence if it was not repaid. I rang several other people who owed me money and subjected them to the same treatment. There I was with £90,000 in a bag ringing people up and threatening them over little more than loose change. It wasn't about the money; it was just me being angry about having to die before my time.

The plan had always been to retire at fifty and enjoy the rest of my life, not retire at fifty and die a year or two later. I couldn't let it happen. I didn't care what the doctors told me; however grim the diagnosis, Wayne Barker was not going to be beaten. I might go down on one knee, I might even kiss the canvas, but rest assured I will get back onto my feet, dust myself down and continue the fight. I won't be beaten by this cancer. I have to keep on believing that, because at this moment in time that belief is my only hope of survival.

ROUND TWO

Born Fighter

I WAS BORN in a two-bedroom flat on Peru Street in Higher Broughton, Salford. My father, Eric, wasn't present at my birth. He was otherwise engaged, serving an eight-month prison sentence for various driving offences. My mother, Mary, started to give birth to me at approximately 5.30 a.m., alone in the flat. Aged just 20, she was petrified at the thought of delivering me. But, as usual, my mother just got on with the task in hand. I entered the world via the kitchen floor and to the sound of my mother hammering on the wall of a neighbour with a poker as she begged for assistance.

My mother was used to adversity. Born in north Manchester, she had eight brothers and sisters, but her mother had deserted them when she was very young. Their father was away fighting for his country during the Second World War, so he was unable to care for them. My mother, who was the eldest girl in the family, took on the role of her absent mother. The parentless children couldn't afford rent and so they lived in bombed-out houses and off the charitable kindness of their community. When the war ended, my grandfather returned to Manchester and took over as the head of his family. My mother's education had suffered as a result of her having to look after her siblings. However, when her father

29

was given a council house she was able to attend school and enjoyed two or three years of normal childhood. When my mother was 15, she left school and worked in factories making shoes and handbags. A year later she met my father.

They say opposites attract, and so it was with my parents. My father had nothing whatsoever in common with my mother. He and his family were villains. His father, Potty Barker, had served an eight-year prison sentence during the war. When he was released, he earned a living running taxis, prostitutes and pretty much anything else that would fund his insatiable gambling habit. At the end of the war, Salford docks became a hive of activity as raw materials and other goods were imported and exported to replenish countries that had suffered heavy bombing raids and land battles. My grandfather and many other men would steal lorryloads of blankets, food and clothing from the docks and sell them to shopkeepers and warehouses in the Salford area. My father tried to emulate his father, but he never did quite have the same energy and wilful attitude. Don't get me wrong, my father was no fool; he just wasn't as keen or as astute as my grandfather.

Life at home with my parents was far from idyllic. There were two children during our time at Peru Street, me and my sister Lorraine, who was fifteen months my junior. Being male and the elder sibling, I bore the brunt of my father's unwarranted, mindless violence, although my mother also suffered at his hands. When my father wasn't in prison, he was buying and selling cars and contraband to fund his social life. During one of my father's many prison sentences, I can recall my mother and I going to what used to be called the Unemployed Assistance Benefits Office. This was housed in a prefab building directly opposite HMP Strangeways. I was about five years old and vividly remember sitting amongst people who were clearly desperate and morally defeated. I have no idea if my mother got the cash handout that she went there for, but the experience, the dire atmosphere of that dreadful place, has never left me. I would rather starve than put my hand out and beg for charity.

One of my earliest memories is of my mother fighting with a prostitute named Helen and my father taking on three men at the same time in the street where we lived. I don't know why it happened. I just know that the police arrived and kept all parties apart until order was restored. A few weeks later, my parents bought a house, 59 Stowell Street in Salford, and we moved in shortly afterwards.

Within a year, my youngest sister, Tracy, was born. I have a vivid memory of my mother going into labour in the middle of the night. The house soon filled with people as grandparents, cousins, uncles, aunts and a midwife arrived to greet the new addition to our family. Lorraine and I sat on the stairs together listening for signs of our sibling who was being born in the front room.

Tracy's arrival made my life somewhat more difficult. My father seemed to hold me responsible for everything that any of his children did. I was the eldest and therefore I should have known better than to allow my sisters to hurt themselves when playing or do anything wrong. Lorraine was the classic middle child; she had an elder in me to blame and a minion below her to blame. Tracy was an infant and therefore could not be held responsible for anything. While she was still a toddler, Tracy pulled the sawdust stuffing from a doll; it got into her eyes and caused permanent damage. This disability meant that the level of blame I shouldered for her misdemeanours was greatly increased.

At the age of five, I was sent to St Ambrose Church of England School on Liverpool Street but I knew from the outset that an orthodox education was not for me. The domineering, power-crazy teachers and their ultimatums reminded me of my bullying father. I hated them and they hated me. In fact, hate was the only thing we had in common. My disruptive behaviour regularly resulted in me being subjected to corporal punishment. I would be shaken, slapped hard around the face and head or my legs would be thrashed, but I never did feel any pain. All I felt was a seething resentment for my tormentors.

At home, things were slightly different. I resented my father's violence because I felt pain, extreme pain in fact, and as I was growing his ferocity intensified. I received my first severe beating one Sunday morning during an Easter weekend. My mother used to bake cakes and, like all children, I would pick at whatever she was making as I walked by. On this particular occasion, my sister Lorraine saw me and made an insulting remark. Lorraine had really long hair, and in retaliation I decided to test out my hairdressing skills and cut all of her flowing locks off. Lorraine began shouting and crying, and moments later my father appeared. He stormed into the lounge and called for me to go to him. When I entered the room, he was sitting in the corner in his chair. 'Come over here, you,' my father bellowed. As I walked towards him, he leaned back slightly and then kicked me as hard as he could in the face. I literally flew across the room before landing in a heap. My nose was pouring with blood and both my eyes swelled up badly. As my father got to his feet, my mother got between us in order to protect me, but he just began punching her instead.

It was becoming increasingly obvious to me that my mother was growing tired of my father's violent behaviour, and I think he knew it too. In an effort to save his marriage, my father did his best to appear apologetic and civil. He even went so far as to secure legitimate employment, driving lorries for a local company called Ordsall Haulage.

On the surface, things appeared to be improving for our

family, but, unbeknown to my sisters and me, the damage had already been done and our parents were preparing to separate. One day we were all living under the same roof and the next my parents had parted and my sisters and I had been placed in foster care. I am not sure how I felt about being removed from my home. The people looking after my sisters and me were kind and considerate, but they were still strangers. I was pleased to be away from the madness, but I still missed us all being together. I have no idea how long we were in care; it was certainly months rather than years.

I do, however, vividly recall the day my mother came to collect us. She was really excited and said that she had found a new home for us all, 133 Queens Road, Cheetham Hill, Manchester. When my mother said 'us all', I assumed she meant me, my sisters and her, but when we arrived at the property my father was there too. Without consultation or explanation, our parents had somehow been reunited.

Lorraine and I were sent to the Temple Junior School on Cheetham Hill Road and for a time life at home was relatively normal. That was until my father's younger brother Jimmy moved into a house not far from our own. At the rear of our house, there were several garages for residential parking, but these were used in the main by my father and Jimmy, who would strip stolen cars of their more valuable parts. The theft of a motor vehicle produces a victim, and not all victims go to the police – some seek revenge. And so it was with a group of Greek men who discovered that a family member's stolen car had passed through the hands of Jimmy and my father. One day, my mother, sisters and I were sitting in the lounge, which was at the front of our house. We all jumped when we heard a bang and the window at the rear of the house shattered. At first, I thought that somebody must have kicked a football through it by accident, but in an instant it became clear that somebody was raking the house with gunfire. My mother screamed, grabbed my sisters and me, and ran through the front door to the safety of the street. Huddled behind a car, we waited until the gunfire had ended and our street was awash with anxious-looking policemen. My father did his best to look bewildered when asked who might want to shoot him, but I very much doubt that anybody believed him.

One evening my father gave me a £5 note to go to the shops and get him a packet of cigarettes. Giving a £5 note to a child back then would be the equivalent of handing over a £50 note these days. I remember that it was cold, raining and dark as I slipped out of the front door with the money held tightly in my hand. When I arrived outside the shop, a boy in his teens asked me how I was and what I was doing. I didn't know the boy; I thought he was just being friendly. I explained that I had been sent to the shop to buy cigarettes for my father. The boy said that because of my age the shopkeeper wouldn't serve me but that he was willing to buy the cigarettes on my behalf. I gave the boy the £5 note, which he folded neatly before putting it in his top pocket and running away.

I imagine that there is still an indented impression of my father on the ceiling of 133 Queens Road, because when I told him what had happened he hit the roof. Grabbing a bullwhip, he began lashing me repeatedly. Using the alphabet as a guide, he screamed an obscenity with each painful strike: 'Arsehole, Bastard, Cunt.' Hearing the commotion, my mother ran in from the kitchen and dived on top of me to protect me from the whip. But that didn't stop my father; he just whipped my mother instead. When the beating had ended, my father dropped the whip and walked out of the room. As I lay on the floor with my mother still shielding me, I felt genuine hatred for my father.

'Why do you put up with this?' I asked.

'I don't know. He beats us and cheats on me with other women. I really don't know,' my mother replied, before breaking down.

My father's violence, blatant infidelity and general lack of care for anybody other than himself devastated my mother. There would be rows, reconciliations, rows and further reconciliations, but nothing would ever change. I remember my mother walking from Cheetham Hill to Wythenshawe one evening in order to find my father. It is a journey of more than 12 miles, so when my mother arrived at the house she believed my father was in, she was far from pleased. The house belonged to my father's friend Alan; he was the brother of Helen, whom my mother had fought in the street. Alan and his friend Bobby were two of the three men my father had taken on in the same incident. Barging into the house, my mother discovered my father with his latest girlfriend and immediately punched her. Instead of showing guilt or remorse, my father grabbed my mother and began beating her in front of his girlfriend and friends. When she had been battered senseless and was bleeding, my father dragged her from the house and threw her into his car.

This car, a 1959 Humber Super Snipe, meant more to my father than anything. It would be fair to say it was his pride and joy. He had acquired it in 1960 on credit but had failed to pay a penny. As they drove away from the house, my father began backhanding my mother hard in the face. When she began to scream and cry, he became more irate and shouted about my mother's blood messing up his car. Sobbing uncontrollably, my mother was unable to reply. When the speeding car reached 80 mph, my terrified mother opened the door and leapt out. As soon as she hit the tarmac, she bounced back into the air and was then tossed along the street before coming to rest by the kerb. My father slammed on the brakes and after checking for signs of life he summoned an ambulance, which took my mother to a nearby hospital.

When doctors examined her, they discovered that she had suffered two broken arms, two broken legs, a fractured skull, damage to her spine and numerous cuts and abrasions. Nobody knows how she survived. After a week, my mother arrived home still in plaster and heavily bandaged. I later learned that she was so concerned about the welfare of my sisters and me that she had discharged herself against the advice of the hospital staff.

A few days later, Lorraine and I were taken to a children's convalescent home in Colwyn Bay, North Wales. We were not sent to this home because of our behaviour, and as far as I know neither of us was ill or had been ill. It was therefore a mystery to us both why we ended up there and remains so to this day. I don't know what if anything happened to Tracy; being so young, she may have stayed in Salford with my mother. The home was divided into two separate sections, boys and girls. Lorraine was naturally upset to be separated from me, as was I to be kept from her, but we would still see each other on occasion.

I have two distinct memories of my time in Colwyn Bay. The first is of being in the dining room eating breakfast, passing wind and without warning soiling myself. I immediately ran from the room to the toilets, clutching my backside. The other children howled with laughter, which only added to my acute embarrassment. Once safely locked behind a cubicle door, I did my best to clean myself, but I was in such a state I was forced to ask a member of staff for assistance. My second memory is of fighting a boy in my dormitory one Sunday morning. I don't recall how or why the fight started. I just remember that during the struggle my pyjama bottoms fell down and I ended up holding the pyjama cord with one hand and trying to punch with the other.

Approximately two months after we arrived at Colwyn Bay, Lorraine and I were informed that we were going home. I'm not sure how I felt. Lorraine was visibly excited, but I had my reservations. I was able to work out that whatever promises my parents had made to each other it was unlikely that anything would actually change. Unsurprisingly, events proved me to be correct. My mother and I were soon getting battered again by my father for little or no apparent reason.

When he wasn't employing violence to control his wife and children, my father was using it to influence relatives, friends and foes. Following the breakdown of his parents' marriage, my father fell out with his own father, Potty Barker. Aged 54, Potty had taken a new, 17-year-old mixed-race partner in place of his wife. My auntie had shown her disapproval of this mismatch by beating the 17-year-old around the head with a poker. The assault resulted in the girl receiving several stitches and various family members taking opposing sides. My father chose to support his mother and his poker-wielding sister. This was no ordinary family dispute. Death threats were issued and both sides armed themselves in preparation for an all-out war. Potty, his brother Herbert, two brothers named Tony and Jimmy and two other men arrived in Manchester one afternoon looking for my father.

When word of the gang and their murderous intentions reached our house, my father armed himself with a .410 shotgun and sat in the lounge to await their arrival. The gang didn't bother knocking when they did arrive. Potty kicked the front door open and crossed the threshold into the hallway. As he did so, my mother screamed and leapt from her chair. My father, who was sat facing up the hall, levelled the shotgun at his own father and went to open fire. My mother, who was still screaming, knocked the barrel of the gun into the air with her arm. There was a deafening explosion and the blast blew a huge hole in the ceiling. As plaster and paint showered down upon us, we could see through the gaping hole that my sister Tracy's cot had narrowly missed being obliterated. Realising my father was intent on using the shotgun, my grandfather and his associates turned and fled. My father jumped up, reloaded the weapon and ran out into the street after them. As the fleeing men made their getaway through nearby gardens, my father fired at least three more shots, which fortunately failed to hit their intended targets.

In no time at all, the street was swarming with police and my father was arrested. Later the same day, he was charged with attempted murder and being in possession of a firearm with the intent of endangering life. When my father eventually stood trial at Manchester Crown Court, Judge Edward Steel threw out the charge of attempted murder on the basis that my father was defending himself, his family and his property. Judge Steel told my father that he had been in his own home, 'presumably minding your own business, when you came under attack from a group of men. You have the absolute right in such circumstances to defend yourself in any such manner as you see fit.' For possessing the shotgun with the intent of endangering life, my father was imprisoned for 12 months.

The volatile environment at home had had a real impact on me. At school, I tended to mimic my absent father. I would use my fists rather than my mouth to communicate with my fellow pupils. After teachers gave me numerous 'chances' to reform, which I ignored, I was threatened with expulsion. My mother thought that her father might have a sobering effect on me, so she asked him to speak to me about my increasingly unruly behaviour. To his credit, my grandfather did try his best, but I have to concede that, despite my tender age, long before I left primary school

Wayne Barker's way was always going to be the only way in his life. I was bloody-minded and stubborn, and nobody was ever going to change that.

Walking home from school one day, I saw my mother pushing Tracy's pram down the street. On the pram were boxes and alongside my mother was my sister Lorraine. Without a word being spoken, I feared the worst: my mother was leaving me. I burst out crying and ran towards her. I begged her not to leave, and she explained that she had in fact been looking for me. She said that while my sister and I had been away in Colwyn Bay she had worked hard and managed to save £200. Since then she had managed to save an additional £100. For the meagre sum of £300, my mother had managed to purchase a two-bedroom terraced house, 18 Bennett Drive, Higher Broughton, Salford. 'There's no need for you to return home. I have all of your clothes here,' my mother said. Another new beginning, another fresh start. I really wanted to share my mother's dream, but deep down I knew that if we were not relocating to the moon nothing would ever really change.

After moving to Higher Broughton, I soon made friends with several older boys. One evening me and one of these boys got into the grounds of a factory at the rear of my home via a hole in the fence. We looked around and eventually found a large ornamental Indian elephant. The older boy told me that we would be able to sell it, but first he would have to find a buyer. He said that I should remain with the elephant until he returned, and I agreed. There's not a lot you can do to pass the time of day with an ornamental elephant, and I soon became bored. It was hardly going to run away, so I went home, picked up some packaging, returned, wrapped up the elephant and made off with it.

I began knocking on doors, asking housewives if they wanted to buy the elephant. Had it been a statue of George

Best, it might have attracted more interest, but Indian elephants don't, I quickly learned, quite capture the imagination of the average housewife in Salford. After knocking on several doors and receiving negative responses, I contemplated changing my sales pitch. Still deep in thought, I knocked on a door and was immediately brought to my senses when Mrs Lavin, a close friend of my mother, answered.

'Hello, Wayne, what can I do for you?' she asked.

'My mam said you wanted to buy this elephant,' I lied.

Raising an eyebrow, Mrs Lavin said that she had no interest in purchasing an elephant but she was going to see my mother to find out what exactly was going on. Mrs Lavin was not the only woman to contact my mother. Before she arrived at my house, several other women had visited my mother enquiring if everything was all right, as they knew my father was in prison. 'Are you short of money? We're only asking because your Wayne's been around trying to sell an elephant,' they had said.

As I was walking up the street with the now partially wrapped elephant that I didn't quite own, I saw my mother and half a dozen other women marching towards me. I was asked where I had acquired the elephant, but I refused to answer. After I'd maintained my silence for some time, my mother frogmarched me to the nearest police station, where I was made to deposit the elephant on the enquiry counter. My mother told the duty sergeant what she knew and I was put behind bars for the first time in my life while the police 'conducted their enquiries'. I was frightened by my environment, but I didn't want to show it, so I began hurling abuse and threats at the officers.

'You're dead when my father gets out of prison,' I shouted at the sergeant.

'I have heard it all before, son,' the policeman replied.

An hour later, I was released without charge and without my Indian elephant. My mother lectured me on the pitfalls of crime, using my father's imprisonment as a shining example of why I should avoid getting into trouble. I gave the impression that I was listening, but, like any adolescent boy, I thought that I knew best.

The only thing I did learn from that particular experience was that my mother was struggling and needed money. I was genuinely horrified that so many women had automatically assumed what I had not even noticed. I decided that, as my father was absent, I would have to take over his role as provider for my family. I started work unloading lorries, helping milkmen with their deliveries and basically doing anything that would bring in some much-needed cash.

When we had moved to Higher Broughton, I had started school at Brentnall Primary, just off New Bury Road. Despite my unruly behaviour in school, I was quite an intelligent pupil and would often finish my work long before my classmates. Inevitably, I would become bored, disrupt the other pupils and find myself in trouble with the teacher. Back in those dark days, corporal punishment was still an option and I was regularly beaten with the strap or the cane for what I considered trivial misdemeanours.

My relationship with my fellow pupils also suffered. After school, Lorraine and I would walk Tracy home because of her visual impairment. The other boys saw this as a non-masculine act and they would call me names. Lorraine and I would often end up fighting three or four boys at a time while Tracy stood by crying with fear.

One morning a casual associate of mine named Gary was playing football in the school yard. I asked him if I could play too. 'Only if you beat those two kids up for me,' he replied, pointing at two notorious bad lads who were glaring at him. These two brothers had recently been returned to school after spending time in a secure children's home. They were constantly fighting and the children in the local area feared them. Without giving the task much thought, I approached the brothers and immediately began punching them. The fight, if it could be called that, was over in seconds. The brothers were left lying motionless on the ground. I walked back to where Gary stood open-mouthed and began to play football.

When I later reflected on what I had done, it occurred to me that I should have just battered Gary and grabbed his ball off him rather than taking on two alleged fighters. But that was me at that time. A lot of people were starting to use Wayne Barker and it would take more than a decade before that situation would change.

Defeating these brothers resulted in many boys wanting to fight me. Some were loyal to them and wanted revenge; others thought that if they were able to defeat me they would inherit some sort of reputation. Whatever my opponent's plan happened to be, it never bore fruit, because I hammered with ease every boy who dared to fight me.

It didn't take me long to realise that I actually loved fighting. The nervous tension before a battle, the physical struggle and then that indescribable rush of adrenalin when an opponent hits the floor and remains down excited me. I revelled in every moment of every encounter, and why wouldn't I? I had been raised in an environment where I had always been the victim. I was now the aggressor and victorious.

Children who are disruptive at school are regularly told by teachers that they will never amount to anything. However, some children admire or respect their disruptive classmates because they see them as revolutionary types, boys and girls who dare to defy authority. Before long, the disruptive child has a following of 'friends' who heap praise on them and so he begins to believe that he is somehow succeeding or achieving. As his ego expands, so too does his circle of 'friends' and a gang of sorts is formed. The disruptive child suddenly becomes a 'somebody' – something his teachers have constantly told him he can never be.

And so it was with me, I became the 'top boy' in school and one of the most feared in the local area. I found the more outrageous my behaviour, the more my classmates would look up to me. I smashed crates full of milk bottles all over the school car park in the hope that the glass would puncture the teachers' car tyres, and I trashed the school gardens. With the benefit of hindsight, I know that nobody was really impressed by my behaviour, nor were the other children really my friends. They feared me too and were simply feigning friendship in the hope that they wouldn't become my next victim.

At the age of 11, I was sent to North Salford Secondary Modern School (which singer Elkie Brooks had also attended, although back then she was known as Elaine Bookbinder). When you leave primary school to attend secondary school, you go from being among the most senior pupils at one establishment to among the most junior at the other. Nobody apart from the children who had attended my primary school knew of my reputation and so I did feel quite wary in my new environment.

There was a big overweight lad named John who seemed to take an interest in me, and I just knew that it wouldn't be too long before we came to blows. John came from a privileged background; he lived alone with his father but wanted for nothing. We were due to have a sports lesson one afternoon, but the weather was particularly bad, so Mr Page, our form teacher, suggested that we all go to the gymnasium. We were split into two teams and told that we were going to box. I don't know why, but I have always believed that Mr Page deliberately selected the teams so that I would have to fight John. Neither of us had ever boxed before and ours was to be the last bout. Throughout the preceding fights, we eyed each other across the ring and a really heavy atmosphere could be felt around the room. Nothing had ever been said, but everybody was clearly aware of the testosterone tension that existed between us.

A loud cheer greeted John and me as we were called into the ring. As soon as we were told to box, I was on my opponent, hitting him hard and fast in the head and body. Ducking and weaving around the ring, I prevented John from landing a single punch on me, so eventually he turned his back in the hope that I would stop hitting him. Before I could inflict any serious damage on John, Mr Page stepped in between us and stopped the fight, declaring me the winner. I came out of that ring feeling twice as tall as when I had entered it. I oozed confidence as I made my way back to the changing-room amid rousing cheers from my fellow pupils.

Within a week, I had fought and defeated the top boy in the second year of the school, and shortly afterwards his counterparts in the third and fourth years had also been humiliated. A kid called Tony was the top boy in the entire school at the time, so it seemed inevitable that we were going to have to fight at some stage. I had publicly refused to recognise his supposed superiority and he had told my friends that he considered me to be no more than a little boy with an overinflated ego. He and his entourage of sidekicks would bowl down the school corridor flashing menacing grins at me in the hope that I would be intimidated.

One morning I stopped Tony as he went to walk past and said, 'Are you the cock of the school?'

'I am,' he replied.

'After school, me and you on Manley Park,' I said.

Tony laughed and said that he would be there.

When I arrived at the park after school, there must have been at least 300 excited children waiting to watch the fight. Tony was jumping around, playing up to the crowd. As soon as he saw me, he crouched as if ready to pounce. I just kept striding towards him and when he was within striking distance I unleashed a barrage of punches. Tony was stronger than me, so I kept my distance, punching, stepping back and then punching again. I caught him on the temple with a blistering right-handed punch and he fell to the ground. As he tried to get up, I hit him again as hard as I could with my right hand and he fell backwards onto the ground, where he remained. That fight, in front of so many people, was an extremely significant event in my life. I truly believed from that moment that no man was better than me and no man ever could be. I firmly believed that I was capable of winning against anybody, whatever the odds.

Having defeated the best that the pupil population could offer, I found myself in regular disputes and confrontational situations with the teachers. Following some sort of misdemeanour, the headmaster Mr Fish was trying to give me six lashes of the cane, but every time he tried to hit me I moved my hand. Mr Fish grabbed my right hand with his left hand and once more raised the cane. With my free hand, I snatched it from him and said, 'What about me giving you the cane?' Before he could reply, I began whipping him across the arms. Mr Fish began screaming for help and within seconds two teachers had come to his aid. They soon disarmed me and I was escorted from the school premises with a stark warning not to return unless I was in the company of my parents.

My father had not been out of prison very long and seemed intent on atoning for his long history of bad behaviour. Relative peace had been established at home and for my mother's sake I wanted things to remain that way. I knew that if I told my father about my bad behaviour a mandatory beating would follow, and that might well result in the destruction of the domestic bliss that my mother was enjoying. Instead of telling my parents that I had whipped the headmaster, I began to get up in the morning, get dressed for school and leave at the usual time. Rather than make my way to school, I would go to work at Lancashire Dairies in Derby Street, Cheetham Hill, where I unloaded and loaded lorries. With my wages, I used to buy my mother a box of chocolates every day. I will never forget the brand she loved; they were called Weekend Chocolates. They were made by Mackintosh's and cost three shillings (fifteen pence) a box. I never told her how I was able to afford such a luxury, and she never asked.

There was a nightclub near our home called the Devonshire and I had noticed that a boy was always hanging around there. Late one night, I escaped from my house via the bedroom window and asked the boy what he was up to. When he replied that he was minding cars, I enquired what that entailed.

'It's simple. As soon as a guy pulls up in his car, I ask him if he wants me to look after it. If he agrees, he gives me money when he comes out of the club, so long as the car isn't damaged. Those that tell me to fuck off usually find that their car has been scratched.'

'Oh, right. That's easy enough. I can help you do that,' I replied.

The boy was probably bored hanging around the streets late at night on his own, and so he agreed. I worked the following weekend with him and we both earned £6. When he arrived for work the following Friday night, I informed him that our partnership was no more and that he was no longer needed. The boy was older than me and refused to take me seriously until I punched him hard in the face. He fought back for a short while, but then he ran off down the street, issuing threats and warning me that he would be back.

Looking after cars turned out to be quite a lucrative and trouble-free pastime. My income doubled and my former partner never did return. While working outside the Devonshire Club, I became acquainted with a Traveller named Johnny Ward. He seemed to admire my desire to work and would often pass on money-making tips. Johnny earned the majority of his income from scrap metal. He pointed out to me that nearly every property in Cheetham Hill had cast-iron drainpipes and guttering. A few days later I was smashing the cast iron with a hammer and collecting the bits in a sack. I would then take the sack of metal to a nearby scrapyard in a wheelbarrow. I wasn't yet in need of an accountant, but with the money I was paid at the dairy and the Devonshire Club I was earning more cash in a week than most grown men.

When I arrived home one afternoon, my mother called me into the kitchen. I thought she had made me something to eat or wanted to know if I was going back out, so I was caught by surprise when I found her clutching a letter from my school. 'Would you like to explain what you have been up to for the past six weeks before your father gets home?' she asked. I told my mother about trying to flog Mr Fish with the cane and about the work that I had been doing since. I quickly pointed out that my employment had funded her daily box of Weekend Chocolates. After much thought, it was agreed that she would visit the school without my father's knowledge on the condition that I behave in the future. I think it was my mention of the chocolates that swayed her. I was forced to make a humiliating apology to Mr Fish and give a solemn promise to behave before I was finally reinstated at school.

Having had a taste of the real world, I was never going

to settle back in at school. To me, the teachers were mugs who had spent half of their lives at college or university in order to earn less in a week than I could in the same period hustling out on the streets. I had simply lost all respect for them and their ideals. When Mr Page, my physical education teacher, tried to humiliate me in front of my classmates by making derogatory remarks about my attempt to cane Mr Fish, I wasn't having any of it. I got up off the bench I was sitting on, walked over to him and kicked him as hard as I could between the legs. As he fell in slow motion to the floor, his face turned crimson red and he sounded as if he was gasping for air. 'And fuck you too,' I said, before leaving the room.

The following day, I went into school and was immediately summoned to the headmaster's office. I was told that in light of a serious allegation of assault upon a member of staff I was not going to be allowed into any classroom. A letter had been sent to my parents telling them to contact the school as soon as possible and until they had done so I would have to do my work outside the headmaster's office. I didn't reply. I just sat at the desk that had been placed directly outside the door to his office.

At ten o'clock the same morning, I was surprised when a teacher came to collect me for swimming. I didn't mention the restrictions that had been imposed upon me and made my way to a local pool with the other pupils. After swimming, I was using a coin-fed hairdryer when a teacher gripped me by the sideboards. I could take being told off by teachers, even being caned by them if it was justified, but one thing I could not and would not accept was people trying to humiliate me. I had done no wrong and if the teacher gripping my sideburns wished to speak to me he certainly didn't have to manhandle me in order to get my attention. As he pulled harder, I twisted my body so that I was facing him and landed a crushing blow straight on his chin. The momentum of my swing sent him flying backwards down a flight of stairs. When I looked down at his motionless body, I really thought that I had caused him serious injury, so I immediately left the swimming baths and made my way home.

Fortunately for me, my father's friends were visiting him and I knew that they would laugh and joke if they heard I had knocked out a teacher. Had my father been alone, I don't think I would have dared face him.

'I think you had better get yourself down the school, Dad. I might be in a bit of trouble,' I said as I entered the room.

'What do you mean? What's gone on?' my father replied.

When I explained how I had assaulted the teacher, two of the men, Curly Lowe and Gypsy Joe, burst out laughing and thankfully my father joined in too. My father, Joe and Curly then got into a car and drove to the school, where they were informed that the teacher had been admitted to hospital. The school had not yet established how the teacher had sustained his injuries, other than the fact that Wayne Barker was somehow involved.

Less than an hour after departing, Curly, Joe and my father arrived back at the house. 'The kid's got to go,' Curly announced as he walked through the front door. I was reasonably sure that the phrase didn't mean that I was going to be executed, but otherwise I had no idea what the trio were planning to do with me. My father asked Curly where he was thinking of taking me and Curly replied, 'Burton's. Take him to Hughie Burton's.'

There was then a general discussion between my father and his friends about the career opportunities that Hughie Burton might be able to offer me.

'He will teach the lad to fight,' said Joe.

'And he'll learn how to ride horses,' added Curly.

Hughie Burton, it transpired, was a Gypsy who lived on

a site in Partington, south-west Manchester. Unbeknown to me at that time, Hughie had kidnapped Curly, Joe and numerous other men from around Manchester in 1958. The men had been taken against their will to the Breidden Hills in Powys, Wales, where they were forced to construct a monument on top of a hill named Moel y Golfa. The monument was erected in memory of Hughie's father, Ernest, whose ashes were scattered there. When the final stones were to be taken up and raised into position, several labourers who were drinking at a pub near Telford in Shropshire were also kidnapped and taken to Moel y Golfa. They were made to complete the final hard work before being freed along with the other prisoners.

After several minutes of discussion between my father and his friends, it was unanimously agreed that I was going to get in trouble for assaulting the teacher and so my best option was to go and live with Hughie Burton on the Gypsy site. At teatime, I was loaded into a car and driven to what was going to be my new place of residence. I had not yet reached my 12th birthday and I was being forced to leave my mother, sisters, father and home. I don't know how I felt; probably nothing, because it didn't seem real.

As we drove towards the site, I could see more than 100 caravans spread out across several fields. Dogs, chickens, horses and children appeared to be running amok. This had to be a ploy to bring me to my senses, surely. I looked around at those in the car with me and nobody appeared to be joking. We eventually pulled up outside a big house on the caravan site. As the car door opened, Curly leaned into the vehicle and said, 'Come on, Wayne, get out. Welcome to your new home.'

ROUND THREE

Travellin' Man

WHEN I GOT out of the car, I saw a huge man sitting outside the house playing an accordion. This was Hughie Burton, whom I later learned was known as 'the King of the Gypsies'. It is a title that many bare-knuckle fighters have attempted to claim as their own in their memoirs, but amongst the Travelling fraternity Hughie's sovereignty is unquestionable. He invited us into the house and listened intently as my father and his friends told him my life story to date. When they had finished, Hughie sat thinking in silence for a while. Then, looking directly at me, he said, 'What do you want?' Curly attempted to speak, but Hughie ordered him to be quiet. 'I asked the boy, not you,' he snapped. I told Hughie that I didn't really know what I wanted. He thought for a little while longer and then suggested that I go away, think about things and return at the weekend. 'Just bring your mother and father, nobody else,' Hughie added.

The mood in the van on the journey home was very subdued. My father and particularly his friends had not enjoyed being in the company of Hughie. He had spoken to Gypsy Joe and Curly with contempt, and the reception my father had received could only be described as frosty. I could understand Hughie not having much respect for two men he had kidnapped and forced into labour, but at the time I didn't know why he had been distant with my father. I later learned that in the early 1960s my father had fought Hughie's brother Oaphie over a music box. Apparently my father had been looking at the box shortly before it had gone missing. Oaphie had put two and two together, come up with five and challenged my father to a fight. In the battle that ensued, my father had been knocked out. Shortly afterwards, Oaphie had found the music box, but no apology had been made.

The way Hughie had spoken to the men in the car with me had somehow excited me. All of my life, my father and to a lesser degree his friends had been powerful people who did as they chose. Yet in the company of Hughie they had been spoken to in the way that they often spoke to me. Hughie Burton was quickly becoming the kind of guy I wanted to be around.

Over the next few days, I spoke to my mother about my future, but I still couldn't reach a decision. When Sunday came, my mother, father and I drove over to the Gypsy site at Partington. Oddly enough, there was no discussion about where I wished to live; the conversation lasted two or three hours and concerned everyday events rather than me.

Then, out of the blue, Hughie turned to me and said, 'What do you want to be, boy? A horse trader, a jockey, a dealing man or a fighter?'

Without hesitation, I replied, 'I want to be a fighting man.'

Hughie said, 'OK. You stay here with me and I will teach you all I can.'

Moments later, my parents were waving goodbye to me and I was left alone in the house with Hughie Burton. He took me upstairs, told me which room I was to sleep in and then left. Despite owning the lavish five-bedroom house, Hughie insisted on sleeping in his trailer (caravan). Tradition was obviously more important to him than comfort.

I suppose I should have been upset, losing my family. The teacher I had assaulted had been discharged from hospital and therefore my punishment would have been only expulsion from school. However, the truth was I was genuinely excited about the prospect of learning to be a man who earned his living fighting allcomers. A romantic notion, my mother would have called it. Perhaps it was just that, but I wasn't going anywhere until I had tried it.

The following morning, I got up early and went outside. It was quite cold, so I was surprised to see Hughie sitting outside his trailer on a bench. After asking how I was, Hughie told me to go and fetch water for the horses; then he showed me how to feed them and the chickens. The horses terrified me at first. They would kick, shit, snort and try to bite me every time I went near them. The only horse I had been near before Hughie's beasts had been made of wood and rocked back and forth.

Not only were the animals pretty intimidating, the other Travellers on the site were too. I felt as if I were an alien that had landed on Earth and the humans couldn't quite work me out. After a couple of days, the children of my age group began speaking to me. One was very keen to know if I could chat girls up. Not wanting to appear unmanly, I told the boy that I could and often did. Young girls in the nearby villages had been warned by their parents to resist advances from boys off the Traveller site, so just being acknowledged by a local girl was considered an achievement. As I was not a Traveller, the boys on the site thought that they could use me as some sort of human magnet to attract the local girls.

That afternoon the Traveller boys took me to the village

and when they saw a group of girls outside a shop they said, 'Go get them, then.'

'Wait here and please don't speak,' I said as I began to cross the road.

I cannot now recall what I said to the girls, but we spoke at length. They had their backs to the Travellers and so I could see that the other boys were watching me almost open-mouthed in wonderment. In hushed tones, I told the girls that I needed them to do me a favour and they agreed. As I strode ten feet tall back towards the boys, one of the girls called out to me, 'Make sure you meet me next week, Wayne!' We had agreed that she would shout it, but the boys didn't know that, and all the way back to the site they were questioning me about my technique, which they believed had secured me a date. It broke the ice between me and the Travellers of my own age, but I was going to need a sledgehammer to crack it with some of the elders.

One day a Traveller called me over to his car and shoved a copy of the *Daily Mirror* into my face. 'Can you read, boy?' he asked. When I said I could, he sat down with me outside his trailer and demanded that I read the racing page for him. I started laughing when it dawned on me that he couldn't read. But my laughter did not last long, because the man realised that I was ridiculing him and knocked me out with a devastating punch that caught me on the chin. When I regained consciousness, he had gone. The following day, however, another Traveller asked me to read his newspaper and I was almost pleased to assist. Again, the man was interested only in the racing page. He wanted to know the form of each horse, the trainer's name and the weather conditions for that day at particular racecourses. I read them to him and, based on what I had said, he chose which horses to place a bet on. Soon numerous men from the site and beyond were calling on me to read the racing page of their newspapers. When they won, I got nothing; when they lost, I would often get punched or slapped. I would never retaliate. I just took it and got on with whatever I was supposed to be doing.

After three or four months, my confidence had grown and my tolerance level was dropping to below zero. One of my regular tormentors was Ted Herne, a 22-stone bully whose favourite thing to say to me was 'You couldn't pick apples off a tree never mind pick fucking horses'. A punch or a slap would usually follow. One day I was sweeping the stables with a heavy-duty yard brush when Herne came storming towards me. 'You gorger-bred [non-Gypsy] bastard!' he shouted. Before he could say another word, I said, 'I am telling you now, you have hit me for the last time.' Herne stopped as if in shock and replied, 'Oh, that's fighting talk, gorger boy.' As he took another step towards me, I swung the brush by its handle so that the heavy head smashed into his skull. He fell to the floor like a sack of shit and remained there. A blood blister the size of a tennis ball emerged on the side of his head, and I thought that I might have killed him. As the other Travellers looked on, I said to them, 'And if any other man wants to hit me, come forward now. Nobody is hitting me any more.' Herne began to groan and struggled to his feet. The only thing I could focus on was the huge lump on the side of his head, which was threatening to explode. Without saying a word, Herne slouched past me and made his way to his trailer.

When Hughie Burton was told what had happened, he came to the stables to see me. I genuinely thought he was going to hit me, but when he walked in he looked at the broken broom and said, 'What's happened to that?'

'I broke it over Ted Herne's head,' I replied.

Hughie looked me up and down, turned and walked away.

That night, I was outside the Greyhound pub in Partington drinking with some of the boys from the site. A 16-year-old Traveller named Webster walked up to me and said, 'I believe you hit Ted Herne today.' When I acknowledged that I had, Webster said, 'So you're a fighting man now, are you?' I have always known when violence is imminent, and I knew Webster's words were leading up to a fight. Not wishing to disappoint, I head-butted him full in the face. When Webster hit the ground, I kicked his head and stamped on his body until I was physically exhausted. What I left when I walked away resembled little more than a bundle of bloodstained rags.

The following morning, I was feeding the horses when Hughie came to see me.

'I heard you had a fight last night,' he said.

'What if I did? The man was asking for it,' I replied.

Hughie didn't mention the fight again, but that afternoon he told me that once I had put the horses away I was to go to the barn. When I arrived, there was a sixteen-year-old boy from Wigan and approximately ten men who were sitting on a circle of hay bales. Hughie called me over and reminded me that when I'd arrived at the site I'd said that I wanted to be a fighting man. 'You hit Herne yesterday lunchtime and battered Webster last night. Are you prepared to fight today?' Hughie enquired. When I said that I was, Hughie told me that I was going to be fighting the teenager from Wigan. I stripped to the waist and the fight began. The boy was older, stronger and more experienced than me, so unsurprisingly I was badly beaten.

Three days later, I fought another boy. My performance improved but I still lost. Hughie asked me at the end of the contest if I still wanted to be a fighting man and I replied, 'Of course.' Less than three hours later, I was stripped to the waist again and facing an 18-year-old man named Emerson. My head was telling me that I could not physically beat this man, but my heart was telling me that I could not lose. From the moment the fight started, I punched, bit, kicked and gouged eyes until Emerson conceded defeat.

I lost my next two fights, but Hughie was determined that I should continue to take people on, because he knew that I was only half the age of some of my opponents and I undoubtedly had ability. He recruited a trainer for me, John Flannigan, who taught me how to elbow, use my head in fights and protect myself. John would bring colliery boys from mining villages in the north of England to fight me. Some fights I would win, others I would lose, but every bout I fought taught me something new.

Despite the fact I was training, I still had to earn my keep. After a couple of months at the site, I had moved out of Hughie's house and into the back of a Transit van, where I slept on a camp bed. Eventually, I was given my own trailer. At 6.30 a.m. every day, Hughie would hammer on the side of my trailer with the flat of his hand until I got up. I would then wash using a cold tap in the corner of the yard, after which I would feed the chickens and collect any eggs that had been laid. There were 20 chicken pens in total, so that particular task took some time. When I had finished sorting the chickens out, I would go to the stables, mix the feed for the horses and then clean and fill their buckets. Hughie would then arrive at the stables to check that everything was in order. Once he was happy that I had done my job, we would go to his trailer for breakfast, which was usually egg or cheese on toast and a cup of tea, prepared by his wife, Esther. Hughie would eat his in his trailer but I would have to go to my own trailer or the barn to eat mine.

After breakfast, I would return to the stables and muck the horses out. I would then brush them down and prepare them for training. Hughie had a half-mile track in a nearby field where each horse would be encouraged to trot for half an hour. I would take one horse out in a trap (a small two-wheeled carriage) and have another on a lead rope behind. That way I could exercise two horses at once. When the horses had finished, I would have to walk them for a while, dry them and clean them, before returning them to their stables.

These chores would take up most of the morning. In the afternoon, I would either be making solid concrete bases for the trailers to park on, doing odd jobs around the site or out in a van with the men trying to earn money. We would collect scrap metal, tarmac drives or cut down trees at residential addresses. Around 7 p.m., we would return to the site for our dinner.

Afterwards me and the other boys would usually gather in the car park to play 'slaps'. This game entailed pairs of contestants stripping to the waist and basically slapping each other across the face and chest until one submitted. The winner would then fight the next contestant. It was a brutal game, but we believed that it taught us to fight. It certainly taught me how to duck and swerve out of the way of flying hands. Alternatively, Hughie would call us all into the barn where we would have to fight one another.

When the weekend arrived, we would go to the Bolton Palais de Dance. It was a popular club that would be bursting at the seams with Travellers from all over the North-west and beyond. The lads from different families and sites would glare across the dance floor at one another and we would always be involved in at least three or four fights each night. The club did have door staff, but they knew that if they intervened in a Traveller dispute then everybody would turn on them, so they pretty much left us to our own devices.

When I wasn't working or socialising, I was being taught how to fight and competing against other young men at least two or three times per week. I knew that Hughie was earning money from the fights I won, so I asked him when I was going to be paid. 'You will get your fair share when you keep winning,' he replied.

There are certain events in the Travellers' calendar that must not be missed, such as the Stow Horse Fair, the Epsom Derby and Appleby Horse Fair. I was on Epsom Downs with Hughie Burton one beautiful Sunday morning waiting for the day's racing to begin. We were in a dip near the finishing line on the inner side of the track where the Travellers used to congregate. Nearby there was a group of non-Travellers who appeared to be looking for somebody. A Traveller named Vinny Clayton asked the men who they were looking for and one replied, 'Well, it's not you, is it?' I considered the response to be insulting, so I offered to fight any member of the group. A big guy, who I later learned was named Johnny Waldron, took his shirt off and said, 'I will take you on for £50.' I threw my money on the ground, took my shirt off and had beaten the man in a matter of minutes.

The following day, we were back at the dip flicking coins for £2 bets. The sun was shining once more, but it was suddenly blotted out as a huge shadow was cast over me. Instinctively, I leapt forward and landed on my feet before turning around. A huge, fat, ugly head was facing me.

'Are you the fucking lad who give it to my man yesterday?' the growling cockney asked.

'And I took his £50,' I replied.

'Well, he is back here today and wants to fight you for a monkey [£500],' the man said.

I didn't have £500, but one of the older Travellers said that he would pay my stake. Moments later, Waldron stood before me and we began to fight. On this occasion, Waldron was better prepared, but I still managed to beat him with a flurry of body punches that left him barely able to breathe.

When I picked up the £1,000, the man mountain grabbed my face with both hands and kissed me on the forehead. 'I like you, son. Lenny McLean's the name. If you're ever looking to earn a few quid, look me up,' he said, before walking away.

Several years after I had defeated Waldron, he fought McLean on two occasions and knocked him out both times. In 1991, Waldron also knocked out Julius Francis, who went on to become the British and Commonwealth heavyweight champion. Waldron turned professional early on in his fighting career, but the BBBC (British Boxing Board of Control) stripped him of his licence because he had a damaged eye.

Similar meetings to Epsom are held in Ireland, such as the Cashel Horse Fair in County Tipperary, the Ballinasloe Horse Fair in County Galway and the Smithfield Horse Fair in Dublin. At all of these events, Travellers gather in their thousands to trade horses, gamble, cockfight and, of course, box bare-knuckle. Hughie said that he wanted me to fight at Smithfield Horse Fair in Dublin, and so late one Saturday night we headed for Holyhead, where we caught the overnight ferry to Dublin. Once we had docked, we drove to Smithfield, where we snatched a few hours sleep in the van. The boy Hughie had chosen for me to fight was in fact a man and, although I gave a good account of myself, I was beaten. With blood still running from my nose, I got back into the van and we were waiting to board the ferry home within the hour.

I think Hughie was just testing the water with me to see how I coped in unfamiliar territory. After that initial trip to Dublin, I would be transported to bouts throughout England,

Scotland, Wales and Ireland to fight, and I soon began winning more than I lost.

When we travelled to Cashel or Ballinasloe, we would take a trailer with us. Rather than use the substandard Irish 'main roads', we would travel from town to town using the lanes, where we would meet other Travellers, as well as tinkers, whom we referred to as 'hedge-hoppers'. The tinkers didn't have trailers to sleep in; they would simply erect a large tarpaulin on the ground, laying one end over a hedge and supporting the other end with poles so it resembled a crude tent. During the day, the tinkers would venture out into the local community to earn what money they could, returning to their makeshift tents at night to sleep. Whenever we parked up at night near to tinkers or other Travellers, Hughie would always try to organise a fight for me. If I won, I would earn approximately £20. Some nights I would fight five or six different opponents, so it could be quite lucrative or very painful depending on the outcome.

On a trip to Appleby Fair, I met a Welsh travelling showman called Vernon Bassett. Showmen earn their living working in circuses, funfairs and amusement arcades. I had been trying to purchase a horse from Vernon, but we could not agree a price. I was only 14 at this time and I think he admired my mature and rather forward attitude. Vernon said that if I ever grew tired of living in Manchester he would find work for me on his fairground in Wales. Despite my outward maturity, I was still a boy at heart, and for weeks afterwards the romantic notion of working on a fairground amidst the music, lights and, of course, girls would not leave me.

Eventually, I succumbed to temptation. I told Hughie that I was off to see a friend, jumped into my pick-up truck and headed for Wales. I got lost several times on the way, but eventually I arrived at a scrapyard owned by Vernon in Caernarfon. I was introduced to his family and told that I could stay with them until I had sorted out alternative accommodation. Initially Vernon put me to work stripping cable at his yard, but when the summer arrived I was employed at fairs and carnivals throughout the country, operating a big wooden swingboat ride or running hoop-la or darts stalls. It was a good experience because it gave me lots of confidence and taught me how to attract and sell to potential customers.

I really enjoyed this period of my life. As well as earning good money, I wasn't fighting every day and I was bedding different girls every night. I certainly learnt more about the real world at those fairs and carnivals than a lifetime at North Salford Secondary Modern could ever have taught me.

I gradually became heavily involved in the whole Bassett family way of life. I loved being around Vernon, his children and his grandchildren. They had a closeness and affection for one another that I had not really experienced before. I still kept in touch with my parents by phone and occasionally I had been to visit them, but the Bassetts were totally unlike the Barkers. I am not implying that my parents didn't care or that my sisters and I were unloved, but I am not sure my father in particular knew how to show affection. The world was undoubtedly a brutal place and he felt he had to prepare us for all that that entailed.

One weekend my father travelled down to Wales to visit me. While he was there, I received a telephone call from my mother, who said that Hughie Burton's son Eugene wanted me to contact him. When I rang Eugene, he said that he had just got married and was going to Scotland on his honeymoon the following morning. 'I want you to come with me to train and race my horses,' Eugene said. I agreed, without giving his request much thought. I had sold my pick-up and so I asked my father if he would give me a lift back to Manchester. My father was driving a Mini Clubman, so by the time I had loaded it up with my possessions there wasn't much room for either of us. I said my goodbyes to the Bassett family, and then my father and I squeezed into our seats to set off back to Manchester.

I don't know what it is with me and cars, but if I am a passenger I will fall asleep almost immediately. My father wasn't in the best of moods because of the cramped conditions in the vehicle, and so every time I nodded off he would slap me to wake me up. I can recall glancing at the dashboard clock after one particularly hard slap. It was four o'clock in the morning. I couldn't see my face, but my impaired vision indicated to me that my left eye was badly swollen. As soon as I fell asleep again, my father slapped me hard across the face with the back of his hand. I couldn't stand it any longer, and I shouted, 'Stop the fucking car because I am going to punch you to death!'

My father jumped on the brakes and the vehicle came to an abrupt halt. Before my father had turned off the engine, I was out on the side of the road and preparing to fight him. Reaching behind his seat, my father pulled out a large leather strap with a horse's stirrup on the end. As I walked around the car towards him, he lashed me with the strap and the stirrup cut the top of my nose wide open. I was unconscious before I had even hit the ground. My father picked me up, threw me in the passenger seat and calmly drove away.

When I regained consciousness a few minutes later, I realised that I was drenched in blood and my face was an absolute mess. 'You won't fucking fall asleep and you won't get cheeky with me again either, you little cunt. You want to fight me? Who do you think you are, you little cunt?' my father shouted. I couldn't answer. I don't think my father realised just how badly hurt I was. I was barely conscious, my face was twice its normal size and I was in absolute agony. It was a high price to pay for falling asleep by anybody's standards. When I arrived home, my mother was visibly shocked by the state I was in. She didn't have to ask who was responsible. After cleaning my face up the best she could, she made me something to eat.

Later the same morning, Eugene came to pick me up. 'Fucking hell! What's happened to you, Wayne?' he asked when he saw my face. I told Eugene that I had fallen out with my father and spared him the finer details by saying that it was no big deal. After transferring my possessions from my father's Mini into Eugene's van, we set off for Motherwell in Scotland. We parked the trailer at a horse track owned by a man known as Fat Bob Kennedy. For three or four weeks, I worked hard preparing Eugene's horses for races at Hawick, Musselburgh and Bannockburn.

At the end of Eugene's honeymoon, we returned to Manchester. During my absence from the site, Hughie had found a man to do the chores that I had once done. His name was Jimmy. He was 36 years old and a former Army physical-training instructor with a current drink problem. I didn't know it at the time, but when Hughie and Eugene were alone, they had been joking about whose man would win in a fight. Hughie had claimed that Jimmy's age, superior strength and fitness would mean that I would be easily defeated. Eugene disagreed, and he bet his father that if he could get Jimmy and me to fight I would win.

Later that evening, Eugene said to me, 'Do you fancy having a fight tomorrow?'

'No problem. Just let me know when and where,' I replied.

The following morning, I was sitting on a grassed area near Hughie's trailer, eating a bacon sandwich and drinking a cup of tea, when Eugene came over to me and asked how I was feeling. 'Good, very good. Who am I fighting?' Eugene told me that it was Jimmy, the guy who now worked for Hughie. 'But he's a grown man. I'm only 14,' I said. Eugene assured me that I would be fine, but I have to admit I did not share his enthusiasm. To be totally honest, I was terrified, but there was no way I was going to admit that to anybody at that time.

Forty-nine people paid a pound each to watch the fight, and the agreement was that the winner would take all. The fight took place in Hughie Burton's house, in a room that had a solid marble floor. Jimmy was hard work at first because he was so strong, but I managed to keep my distance from him and land well-aimed punches that sent him staggering backwards every time they connected. When I saw that he was tiring, I unloaded a flurry of powerful blows that sent him flying into the fireplace. Realising that victory was mine, I moved in close and punched his head and face as fast and as hard as I could. Somebody shouted, 'He's had enough,' and I called back, 'I'll decide when he's finished.' I hit Jimmy with half a dozen more powerful punches to the head and body, and when he finally fell to the floor I stepped back.

It was a momentous occasion. I could see that many of those in the room were impressed. Few had thought a 14-year-old boy would beat a fit grown man in such a confident and comprehensive manner.

One of the men present at that fight was a 22-stone ex-wrestler named Vinnie Carroll. Vinnie traded in cars but was known throughout Manchester as a villain. The following night, I saw Vinnie at a horse track in Droylsden on the outskirts of the city. He asked me how I was and what my thoughts were about the fight the night before. Bursting with confidence and bravado, I told Vinnie that I had beaten Jimmy without sustaining so much as a scratch. 'You ought to be careful who you fight. You're only a boy,' Vinnie reminded me.

I had agreed to fight one of the jockeys, a man named Mather, at the racetrack later that evening, for £50. He wasn't a particularly big man, but he was 25 years of age. However, it was a no-contest fight. I absolutely destroyed him within a couple of minutes.

The following morning, Vinnie arrived at my father's house and told him that he had to get me away from the Travellers. 'They had your boy fighting a man on Sunday and a man last night. If you don't stop it, he'll end up seriously hurt or dead,' Vinnie said.

Shortly afterwards, my father arrived at the site and told me that I had to return home.

'Why what's up?' I asked.

'Nothing's up. Your mother just wants you home,' my father replied.

Eugene Burton had become like a brother to me, and he asked my father why I had to go home. Dismissing Eugene, my father said that my mother wanted me home and that was to be the end of the matter. Eugene turned to my father and said, 'He has to go home so that you can beat him around the face with a stirrup?' I intervened and told Eugene not to speak to my father in that manner. 'My mother wants to see me. I'll come and see you in the week. Let's leave it at that,' I said.

I put my possessions in my father's car and he drove me home. My father was a little embarrassed about the incident with Eugene. He felt that he had lost face. When Eugene insulted him, he knew that there wasn't much he could do. Picking a fight with a Traveller in the middle of a Travellers' site would undoubtedly be bad for one's health, so my father had not retaliated. It was troubling him, though, so he rang Eugene and said I had now seen my mother and if he wanted to come to the house to pick me up I could return to the site with him. As soon as the call ended, my father said that if Eugene did turn up he was going to shoot him. He rang his most trusted friends and lay in wait to maim or murder the man I had come to look on as my brother. Fortunately for all concerned, Eugene sensed that something was not quite right and chose to ignore my father's invitation.

ROUND FOUR

True North

THE DAY AFTER I arrived home my father said that if I really wanted to fight he would take me to a boxing club and I could learn to do so properly. 'It's all I want to do, Dad. I just love fighting,' I replied.

I had just turned 15 when I first walked into Marchants Gym in Salford. It was a Sunday morning, and my father and his friend Keith Ferguson, a notorious Manchester villain, were with me. The man who greeted us was in his 60s, small in stature and wearing a tie, shirt and cardigan. 'Hello, lads, my name is Albert Marchant. How can I help you?' he said. I had never seen anything like that gym in my life. I was used to seeing big hairy Gypsies swearing, shouting and threatening to knock lumps out of one another. In this gym, the men were quiet, controlled and going about their business methodically. Alan Tottoh, who fought for Great Britain in the 1968 Mexico Olympics, was in the corner of the gym pummelling a punchbag. Over the next few years, Alan became a good friend and taught me how to box rather than spit, scratch and snarl like an animal, which at the time was all I knew about fighting. I have to admit that I was quite taken aback by everything I saw that morning.

While I looked in awe around the gym, my father talked to Albert. After a few minutes, Albert called me over and said, 'Can you fight, kid?' I said that I could and just to emphasise the fact I pointed to two guys who were sparring in the ring and claimed that I could batter both of them. Albert smirked, said OK and told me to put a pair of gloves on.

Terry Dolan, one of the men in the ring, was chosen by Albert to fight me. When the bell rang, I launched myself at Terry, but he just stepped out of the way and jabbed me. For three rounds, I chased him around the ring swinging wildly, but very few of my punches made contact. Terry's jabs, on the other hand, not only connected, they knocked me backwards and made me look rather foolish. The more frustrated I became, the easier it became for Terry to hit me. When the bell rang to signal the end of round three, I was more than pleased.

As I climbed out of the ring, I noticed a man watching me intently. I had never seen anybody suffering from alopecia and so, being just a young boy, I couldn't help but stare. This man was about 60 years old; he had no hair on his head, no eyebrows, no eyelashes and no trace of a beard. 'My name is Matty, in case you're wondering. I'm Albert's brother. We're open to the public Tuesday, Thursday and Sunday. I suggest you come here Monday, Wednesday and Friday if you want to improve,' he said matter-of-factly.

I arrived at the gym the following Monday with my father in tow. He and Albert stood outside the ring while Matty began the process of teaching me the noble art of boxing. 'You have to have snap, lad. It's no good wading in swinging your arms,' Matty said as he bobbed and weaved in front of me. As I stepped forward, he slapped me hard across the face. 'Keep your guard up, lad. You have to protect yourself as well as attack.' By the end of the first lesson, I doubt if I had improved much, but I had certainly learned to make my head as difficult a target as possible.

I became a sponge for all of the immense boxing knowledge that Matty and Albert had amassed over many years. I loved those two old men and I loved every minute that I was in their company in that gym. Boxing became my world. Within just a few months, I had become an entirely different fighter. As well as courage and willpower, I had skill, ring craft and a greater level of fitness.

Full of confidence, I returned to Hughie Burton's site and challenged a 22-year-old respected fighter named Jimmy Boswell. 'On the car park, £100 each, winner takes all' was the reply that I was given. Word spread through the site that I was going to fight Boswell and a crowd soon gathered, believing they were going to witness me take a hiding. As soon as the fight had started, I began boxing the head off Boswell. He swung, lunged and even tried to grab me, but I ducked, weaved and landed blow after powerful blow into his ribs, face and head. The fight was over within two or three minutes. I shook Boswell's hand, collected my winnings and left.

That fight was a defining moment in my life. I had proved myself to my father, I had proved myself to Hughie Burton and the Travellers, but more importantly I had proved to myself that I could act alone. I didn't need my father shouting and screaming at me for motivation. I didn't need Hughie's money to make me fight. I had stuck with the training, I had absorbed the advice, and I had challenged and beaten a respected fighter on my own. It felt as if Wayne Barker the man had finally arrived in the world.

There was a downside to beating Jimmy Boswell: I became a little too confident, to the point that I might have come across as brash or brazen to some people. I foolishly believed that I had learned all I possibly could at Marchants Gym, and so I went in search of trainers who could teach me different techniques and styles. I joined Ardwick Boxing Club in Palmerston Street, which is in the East End of Manchester.

It was there I first met an Irish Traveller named Paddy 'Whack' Ward, who these days calls himself Paddy Doherty. Others who boxed at the gym with Paddy were his half-brother Martin McDonagh and his cousins Chris, Mike and Johnny Joyce. They were the in-crowd at the boxing club, but in years to come Paddy and the Joyce family were to become bitter enemies.

From 2009, Paddy began upsetting the Travelling community by appearing in various television programmes, including *Danny Dyer's Deadliest Men*, *Big Fat Gypsy Weddings* and *Celebrity Big Brother*. Travellers are very secretive about their lives and culture, and some felt that Paddy was not portraying them in a very complimentary light and exaggerating his standing amongst them in the process.

In 2010, after a night out drinking, Paddy was attacked and beaten by Johnny Joyce's 20-year-old son, also called Johnny. Paddy suffered multiple breaks in his jaw, black eyes, a gash to his lip needing 12 stitches and severe swelling to his nose, head and neck. Unfortunately, the matter did not end there; Paddy did the unthinkable and cooperated with the police, whom his wife had called. Johnny Joyce stood trial at Manchester Crown Court, where jurors heard that Paddy had bragged on television that he was a bare-knuckle boxing champion and would 'eat people like bars of chocolate'. According to Paddy, there was a simmering feud after Joyce had assaulted his daughter, his son-in-law and his son-in-law's father at a funeral. Paddy was said to have backed down from the initial confrontation – but the hatred exploded a few weeks later. Paddy told the court that Joyce was armed with knuckledusters and attacked him without warning. He said: 'I remember standing up, searching my pockets for my phone, then it was lights out. I remember getting punched and that was it. I thought it was a dream. I could feel my face going crack, crack, crack and he said, "You're dead now, you bastard." I never saw it coming.'

However, Joyce, in his defence, claimed that he feared Paddy had lured him to his caravan park home to settle old scores and said he was 'frightened for [his] life'. Joyce told the court, 'I thought he was looking around . . . for something to stick in me. I hit him but he tried to get back up, so I hit him a few more times to make him stay down so I could get away.' After deliberating for just one hour, the jury found Johnny Joyce not guilty.

Outside the court, Johnny's father told reporters, 'We deal with things amongst ourselves, we shake hands and we forget about it. What happens now is that we'll keep our end of the bargain, we won't retaliate. If anything happens, it's from that side.' Referring to *Big Fat Gypsy Weddings*, he said: 'It doesn't paint the right picture; it doesn't really portray Gypsies how they really are. But that comes from the Gypsies on the show; they know what they're doing. They're doing it for the cameras. He [Doherty] lives in a fantasy world and everybody was laughing at him on the telly, saying, "Who's he?" That's the way he was seen in the community. He was always trying to give a manly image, that's the truth. But he's a clown. He's like the guy who tried to sell the Eiffel Tower. He dreams and fantasises.'

The war of words continued after the trial. The Joyce family called Paddy a grass and Paddy's son David was arrested on suspicion of threatening to kill Johnny Joyce. In another incident, armed police swooped on a convoy of up to 100 Travellers after being warned that they were on their way to an organised fight between Joyce and Paddy. Cars surrounded the convoy and two helicopters were scrambled after a tip-off about the proposed bout. Three guns were seized and eleven arrests were made after the convoy was intercepted on a council estate in Middleton, Manchester. Johnny Joyce was travelling with the convoy and was searched, but he refused to answer any police questions.

I knew both parties, so I tried to bring about an honourable end to the dispute. I put up £50,000 prize money on behalf of Johnny, and in the *Daily Mirror* newspaper I urged Paddy to find somebody to back him. The fight was to take place at the next Appleby Horse Fair and the winner would collect £100,000. I told the reporter, 'We don't want war-mongering in the community. Let's do it the proper way – the way these people have done it for years – and settle it in the ring. This is Paddy Doherty's chance to redeem himself in his own culture. If he had taken his beating like a man that would have been an end to the story.'

Paddy told the *Daily Star* newspaper, 'We will settle this the traditional way. It is the only way to end it. It's not about money or TV or boxing promoters. It's about settling things once and for all. Johnny Joyce is a sausage. When he went for me I'd been drinking for three days. I'm 30 years older than him. And he hit me when I wasn't looking. That is a disgrace. Next time I will be looking and I will be ready. I am willing to fight to my last breath. I've had to do it before and I will do it again. This time it will be fair and square. It won't be pretty. My grandfather was a fist-fighter. My dad was a fist-fighter. I have done it all my life. The Joyces are not in the same league. They are not proper Travellers. They live in a house. And they have picked on the wrong man.'

A few months later, Paddy was out jogging when he

encountered Johnny Joyce and his brother Dougie. Words were exchanged and a fight broke out. In the battle that ensued, Paddy's ear was bitten and left hanging off. The Joyce brothers were arrested and remanded in custody to await trial. While in hospital having his ear stitched back on, Paddy gave a statement to police claiming he had acted in self-defence. He told detectives: 'I was in fear for my life. Johnny Joyce had previously broken my jaw in seven places. I spent some time on a life-support machine. They [the two Joyce brothers] are much younger and bigger than me. I believe they both take steroids. I remain in fear for my life.'

Later the same night, shots were fired outside the Joyce family home. Two men loyal to Paddy, Ryan Ward and Joseph Louthan, were later imprisoned for possessing a firearm with intent to cause fear of violence in connection with the shooting. A week later Paddy's son David was arrested for attempted murder. It was alleged that he had driven over a man's legs in his car before getting out and trying to blast him with a shotgun. The charge was later dropped, apparently because witnesses refused to give evidence. David was subsequently slashed across his back and buttocks after a five-strong mob ambushed him.

Despite Paddy cooperating with the police, the Crown Prosecution Service decided to also charge him with affray following the altercation with Johnny and Dougie Joyce. When the three men appeared in court together, family members fought a pitched battle in the street outside. Dougie Joyce was later sentenced to do one hundred and fifty hours' unpaid work as part of a twelve-month community order; his brother Johnny was imprisoned for fifteen months; and Paddy Doherty was given twelve months' imprisonment, which was suspended for two years.

Paddy moved away from Manchester to a Travellers' site

in Queensferry, North Wales. Remembering how close the Joyce and Ward families were when we all attended the Ardwick Boxing Club makes it hard to believe that they ended up having so much hatred for one another.

I had four amateur fights for Ardwick Boxing Club and won them all, the last being against Chris Joyce. Having done well at Ardwick, I once more felt that I needed fresh trainers, so I moved to the Cavendish Amateur Boxing Club. While there, I won the Amateur Boxing Association junior title.

In 1976, I suffered my first defeat as an amateur when I fought a boy named Jennings in the final of a competition. That defeat made me question my boxing ability for a short while. I couldn't accept losing, but, credit where it's due, Jennings boxed my brains out. He kept well away from me in the ring, jabbing before stepping quickly away. However hard I tried, I just couldn't get close to him.

I had two more amateur fights after Jennings, which I won, but my enthusiasm for the sport had waned somewhat. For beating an opponent, I was being given chest expanders, tea sets, clocks, certificates and trophies. They might have looked good on my mother's mantelpiece, but they weren't worth anything. I needed money, not meaningless trinkets, so I decided to return to fighting men for cash. I travelled to Ireland and fought at Cashel and Ballinasloe horse fairs. My average purse was £100 for a victory and I was fighting three or four times per day.

Despite not having a driving licence, I bought myself another pick-up truck from an auction with my winnings and would go out after training each day collecting scrap metal. I was soon making a reasonable living and often enjoying the thrill of taking what wasn't mine. Where I lived in Salford, there was an area where haulage companies would park their vehicles. I would purchase broken-down lorries from scrapyards and replace their malfunctioning parts with items I had stolen from vehicles on the lorry park. I would then sell the lorries for twice the price I had paid for them. My favourite vehicle was a BMC 550 EFG, which had a rounded front. These particular lorries were extremely popular because of their reliability and engine power and were therefore easy to sell.

I used to visit a scrapyard in Drury Lane, Failsworth, on a regular basis and noticed that adjacent to it was a yard full of steel. The yard appeared to be unoccupied, so another man, whom I'll call Ian Cooper, and I began loading the steel onto my pick-up truck. I can only describe Ian as a fat, brain-dead fool with a driving licence. My father had insisted I employ him to drive me around as I had no licence. I was not happy with the situation, but putting up with Ian was easier than falling out with my father, so I had complied. When we had loaded my truck, we drove to Salford and reloaded the steel onto a lorry I legitimately owned on the lorry park.

After making eight or nine trips, we decided that the next load would be our last for the day. As we were lifting the steel onto my truck, Ian said that he thought somebody was watching us. When I looked around, I could see that there were three police cars all parked in strategic positions and the occupants were indeed watching Ian and me. I told Ian to ignore them, and once we had loaded the steel I set about securing it safely to my truck with rope. When I had finished, I sat in the truck with Ian, drank coffee and had a sandwich. I told Ian that we had to act as though we were doing nothing wrong.

'If we get stopped when we leave here, my name is Joseph Lea and we both live at Mersey House Caravan Site, Hall Lane, Partington. Do you understand that, Ian?' I said.

'Yes, OK, no problem,' Ian replied.

What Ian did not know was that prior to us taking any of the steel I had written out a sales receipt for 30 tonnes. I reasoned that if we were stopped I could at least pretend that I owned the steel. As we went to drive out of the yard, a police car blocked our vehicle's path and an irate-looking officer ordered us to stay in our seats.

'What are you doing with that steel?' the officer asked.

'It's mine. I bought it for £6 per tonne,' I replied.

The officer did not believe me and demanded to see a receipt, which I retrieved from the glove compartment and handed to him. After studying the receipt, the officer asked me for my name and address. I told him I was Joseph Lea and I lived on the Travellers' site at Partington. After walking away to consult with his colleagues, the officer returned to my truck and told me that the man I had purchased the steel from did not own it and never had.

'You have been conned, sonny,' the officer said with a wry smile.

'How do you know he didn't own it?' I replied.

The officer knew exactly what I'd done but he couldn't prove it. What he could do, though, was prevent me from taking away the steel. 'Go back into that yard, unload that steel and then find the man you say you bought it off and bring him to me,' the officer said.

I had eight or nine loads of steel sitting on my lorry in Salford and I wasn't going to be arrested, so I was happy to do what the officer had ordered. As we started to back up, the officer shouted for us to stop and asked Ian his name. Up until this point, Ian had not uttered a word. Gasping for breath and in a state of sheer panic, he blurted out, 'My name is Ian Cooper and his real name is Wayne Barker.'

My fucking head fell off. I could not believe that the bungling barrel of quivering lard sitting next to me had grassed me up. The policeman could not quite believe his luck as he led me to his car in handcuffs. His colleague laughed as he pretended to console Ian, who was by this time weeping. We were taken to a police station and kept in the cells prior to being interviewed. I refused to answer any questions, but Ian gave long, detailed answers to everything he was asked.

When my father arrived at the station, he acted as though he was really shocked that I had been accused of such a thing. 'My lad wouldn't break the law. He's an amateur boxer and would be frightened of losing his boxing licence,' he said. The policeman knew my father, though, so his words fell on deaf ears.

I was later granted bail, but Ian refused to leave the police station as he claimed he feared for his safety. Considering how I felt that day, it was probably a wise move.

When I appeared at Oldham youth court, my mother accompanied me and spoke in glowing terms of my previous good character. The magistrate was suitably impressed and I was given a two-year conditional discharge. This meant that I would not receive any punishment; however, if I reoffended within two years I would not only be penalised for whatever crime I had committed, I would also be punished for taking the steel. Because of his age and the fact that he was driving the vehicle used in the crime, Ian Cooper was seen as a man who had led me astray and was sentenced to three months' imprisonment. And who said there is no such thing as justice?

After the court case, I returned to amateur boxing and trained extremely hard. I had a total of 49 fights, of which I won 44. The pinnacle of my amateur career came on 21 February 1978, when, at the age of 18, I reached the Amateur Boxing Association senior finals. At the time, I was boxing for Greater Manchester Police. Boxing for the police didn't mean that I had seen the light. Police amateur boxing clubs have been in existence since 1928. I imagine that a well-meaning officer thought that encouraging kids like me to learn the noble art might help them to go on to lead well-disciplined, trouble-free lives. That, in most cases, is precisely what happens, but some kids, me included, just love the adrenalin rush that misbehaving brings a little too much.

My father had recently acquired a Daimler Sovereign and insisted on driving me to the fight. On the way, we were listening to the radio and on one station commentators were discussing the forthcoming night's boxing. The presenter announced that the welterweight division, which I was in, had so many contestants that they were going to hold the semi-final and the title fight on the same evening. The commentator added, 'Wayne Barker is due to face fellow Manchester Police Boxing Club member Wayne Crolla, who I believe is too strong for Barker. I think Crolla will knock him out and meet Lee Hartshorn in the final.' My father nearly put his foot through the floor of the car as he jumped on the brakes. Glaring at the radio and then at me, he said, 'If you get knocked out tonight, I will kick you all the way home and then fucking kill you.'

It's fair to say that my father's managerial skills were somewhat lacking in political correctness, but his ability to motivate me was second to none. I can only liken it to the type of twisted encouragement that was meted out to the Colombian national football team. After defender Andrés Escobar scored an own goal in the 1994 World Cup, he was assassinated when he returned to Colombia. A few years later, the Colombian team won their first title when they beat Mexico in the final of the Copa América. Fear makes you try just that little bit harder; you discover energy that you never knew you had.

My father's threats were all I could think of when I

entered the ring to face Crolla. He turned out to be a solid hard-hitter who stunned me more than once, but I was never going to go down. I won the bout on points, but it was a tough fight and I sustained two black eyes. The title fight later that night with Lee Hartshorn was not as punishing; it was extremely close, but I lost on points. I thought the decision could have gone either way, so I asked my trainer to arrange a rematch. Hartshorn displayed true sportsmanship and accepted my offer to fight him again.

It was to be some time before the bout could take place, so I threw myself into a tough training regime during the day and went in search of money-making opportunities at night. One evening I met a scruffy man named Jim Dillon, who used to train alongside me at Marchants Gym. Dillon was literally stinking rich; he had wealth but never bought soap. He had earned his money making concrete fence posts and wooden panels. Dillon knew that I was involved in scrap metal and various other enterprises, and during our conversation he asked if I had any experience of tree-felling. 'Loads. My family have been involved in that game for generations,' I lied. Believing my ridiculous pretence, Dillon went on to explain that he had recently purchased 35 acres of forestry that needed to be cleared. I said that I would be interested in doing the job, so the following day he took me to look at the site, which was in a place called Pendle, near Burnley. The forest was not accessible by car, so we had to travel around it on an old tractor. Dillon told me that he had purchased the trees on the land from the water board. He wanted any tree trunk wider than 5 in. cut down and sawn into 6-ft 1-in. lengths, which he would then use as fence posts. 'I would be prepared to pay you 50p per post,' Dillon said.

We shook hands on the deal and I immediately went in search of two men who would be capable of doing the job.

When I eventually sourced the men, I offered them 25p per post and they accepted. I worked extremely hard twelve hours per day seven days per week alongside the two men. Because of this, I was physically and mentally exhausted by the time the rematch with Lee Hartshorn came around. I am not making excuses; I am merely stating a fact.

The fight was held at Oldham Football Club and while we were waiting to enter the ring Lee said to me, 'No more fights between us after this one, Wayne. We are mates, OK?' I shook his hand and agreed. Lee was a genuine good friend of mine outside the ring; we boxed for the same club and I had been best man at his wedding. The fight was once more decided on points and I lost by a narrow margin. I was disappointed, but I couldn't complain. Lee just edged it on the night.

When the tree-felling job ended, I had earned approximately £30,000 profit. The first thing I purchased was a big American Cadillac Sedan de Ville for my father. I paid £3,000 for it, which was a lot of money back then. It was the first car I had ever seen that had a television in it. My father, who loved cars, was naturally delighted.

While I was looking for the vehicle for my father, I spoke to a car dealer named Peter Wrigley, who had recently been banned from driving. Peter was a family friend and he told me that he was closing down his car pitch and moving over to Canada for a while. 'If things work out, I will stay. If they don't, my driving ban will be up by the time I return and I can start buying and selling cars again,' he said. I told Peter that I wouldn't mind going to Canada and he suggested that I travel with him.

Throughout the long flight, Peter and I were brimming with expectation and hope. We talked about the opportunities a fresh start could offer, but within a week of landing Peter said that he missed Salford and returned home. I am not the type to quit in any situation, so I decided to stay for a while and see what if anything would happen.

I met a guy from Oldham who had lived in Canada for 20 years. He had married a Canadian, joined the police force and reached the rank of sergeant. He was kind enough to let me stay with him and his family in Edmonton, Alberta. I secured a menial job, working with hippies making furniture, which paid $5 per hour. I did this for approximately three months before accepting a job as a doorman at a club called the Warehouse. I worked from 10 p.m. until 2 a.m., but there was rarely any trouble. The clientele were nice, decent people who were only interested in enjoying themselves. As I was only working four hours per evening, I took on two other jobs. During the day, I sat alongside drunks and dossers cleaning reclaimed bricks. For each brick I cleaned, I was paid 75 cents. I would buy cheap bottles of wine and when my fellow workers had cleaned a large pile of bricks I would give them to them. They would disappear in a drunken stupor and I would declare their bricks as mine. I also worked as an usher in a cinema from 6 p.m. until 10 p.m. I didn't have to do a great deal; most of the time I would sit and watch the movies.

I opened an account at the Canadian Bank of Commerce. I can recall sitting in a room with one of the bank staff and she was asking me which type of cheque I would like. Canadian cheques used to have your name and address printed in the top right-hand corner and they were decorated with a variety of images such as flying geese or galloping horses. A week later, I received a parcel from the bank containing ten cheque books, each containing fifty cheques.

I went to the Hudson's Bay store in the shopping precinct and picked out a shirt that cost $20. 'How would you like to pay for that, sir? Cash or cheque?' the sales assistant asked.

I gave her a cheque and explained that I was still waiting for the guarantee card as I had only recently arrived from the UK. She said, 'That's fine, sir, I'll just need your passport number.' Moments later, I had left the store with my new shirt and a huge smile on my face. To ensure that my good fortune had not been a mistake or a one-off opportunity, I walked into a garage and asked the cashier if he would cash a cheque for me. 'Sure, sir, no problem. How much for?' came the reply. I signed the cheque, flashed my passport and walked out of the garage with $50.

I decided that I would use the 498 cheques I had left to fund my time in Canada and when they were all gone I would return home. I hired a huge American car and left Edmonton to find out what fate had in store for me.

I ended up in a place called Saskatchewan, where I heard that they were paying men $12 per hour to work in a uranium mine. The main use of uranium is to fuel nuclear power plants, but the military use it in armour-piercing ammunition. During the latter stages of the Second World War, it was used to produce nuclear weapons. Despite reservations about going home green and glowing, I applied for and was given a job with a company called Eldorado Nuclear in Uranium City. They had a mine called Beaverlodge, which produced uranium for nuclear power plants. It was my job to watch a conveyor belt that transported the ore to the surface. If any oversized lumps of ore found their way onto the belt or it became blocked, I had to remove them or clear the obstruction. I often worked double shifts and was earning an extremely good wage. Unfortunately, the mine was miles from civilisation and so it was impossible to spend any of the money that I was being paid. I had already saved a considerable amount of money from cashing cheques, so it wasn't long before I had several thousand dollars at my disposal. After three months working at the mine, I got into a trivial dispute with an Irishman, whom I knocked out. I was sacked on the spot for gross misconduct and asked to leave on the next bus back to civilisation.

A man named Keith, from Toronto, was also leaving the mine that day and we ended up flying to Edmonton together. I didn't fancy hanging around in Edmonton because of the cheques I had cashed there, so Keith and I flew to a place called Yellowknife in the Northwest Territories. The idea was that we would work at one of two gold mines in Yellowknife but when we arrived there weren't any vacancies.

While Keith scoured the situations vacant columns in the local and national newspapers, I would trawl the local bars for women. One night I met an Eskimo girl named Lena in a nightclub called the Four Seasons. She told me that she was single, lived alone and worked as an interpreter. The thought of living rent-free with a beautiful girl appealed to me, so I launched a full-on charm offensive. After we spent a thoroughly enjoyable evening together, I was invited back to her apartment, which was extremely plush. We had a few drinks, chatted and listened to music before I left to return to the YMCA where I had rented a room.

Lena invited me to dinner the following evening and when I arrived she asked if I preferred fish or caribou meat. Images of Rudolph being butchered swirled around my head, so I opted for the fish instead. Lena went into the kitchen and returned carrying a plate with a raw fish on it. Lena tucked in to the uncooked fish, but each time I looked at mine its dead eye seemed to stare back accusingly at me from the plate. As I gulped down glass after glass of wine, Lena realised that I was never going to touch the fish. Laughing as she led me from the table to her bedroom, she asked if there was anything else I fancied instead. It was two days before

I saw sunlight again. I ended up living with Lena and during our time together I learnt a lot.

I used to go hunting with Keith, shooting muskrats mainly. Very few people other than Indians and Eskimos were granted hunting licences in Canada, so we had to take the large number of animal skins we would accumulate to various Indian reservations to sell. The Indians were being underpaid when they sold them on, so we ended up getting next to nothing for them. Lena explained that the Eskimos were far shrewder and if we sold the skins to them we would get a much better price.

Keith and I went in search of a prospective buyer and soon found ourselves being invited into an igloo which had been built on a huge frozen lake. The first thing that struck me was how warm it was inside. Keith explained to the head of the Eskimo family that I was visiting from England, had no work and needed to sell the skins. As soon as he had mentioned England, the Eskimo looked at me, smiled and began saying, 'English, English,' over and over again. When he had stopped smiling and repeating himself, the Eskimo agreed to buy any skins that we could bring to him.

As we prepared to leave the igloo, the Eskimo summoned a female Les Dawson lookalike and said to me, 'This is my wife. She is for you.' I asked the Eskimo what he meant, but before he could answer Keith had said, 'He is saying that you can sleep with his wife.' I am all for acts of charity, but this was a step too far; the entire 20 stone of this woman was actually quite frightening. Keith said that if I refused the Eskimo's generous offer it would be considered a great insult and we might not leave the igloo in one piece. So, for Queen, country and to ensure we had a customer for our skins, I did the unthinkable and had sex with the Eskimo's wife.

I have since learned that Eskimos often let other men sleep with their wives for various reasons. The most common is a ritual spouse exchange, which is associated with a religious purpose. Another type of wife-sharing is sometimes described as co-marriage. The idea is to strengthen economic and friendship bonds between two families, who can depend on each other in times of need. Most Eskimos have more than one wife, so the practice may not seem as bizarre to them as it might to conventional couples in the UK.

When Keith and I had been travelling from Indian reservation to reservation, I had noticed that quite a few of the Indians appeared to have a drink problem. Off-licences and shops were prohibited from selling alcohol on a Sunday, so Keith and I would spend Saturday afternoons driving around amassing as much alcohol as we were able to store. On Sunday afternoons, we would visit each reservation and sell the alcohol to the Indians at an inflated price. We were never going to get rich, but we made a reasonable living. When you are dealing with drunks, there is always going to be trouble, and after one or two incidents a few of the younger and fitter Indians took an interest in me. It was apparent that they were spoiling for a fight, so I challenged one of them. He accepted my offer and we agreed to fight for a crate of whisky and $60. I supplied the whisky and the Indian put down the cash. I beat him without breaking into a sweat, picked up his $60 and left. News of the bout soon spread around the reservations and before long I was fighting Indians for money on a regular basis.

While drinking in a bar one night, I met a group of students who made a living selling encyclopaedias. They would travel to different towns securing orders from housewives and anybody else they could catch at home. We soon became friends and they would lend me a Volvo they owned whenever I needed to get anywhere. After a while, I not only joined their sales team but also promoted myself to driver, chief cashier and accounts manager. Nobody objected. We would visit a neighbouring town and I would drop the students off so that they could begin the arduous task of knocking on doors to sell the encyclopaedias. Most people would pay cash for the books and when the sales team passed the money to me I would keep it rather than put it in the bank. I knew that their employer would ask questions eventually, but I didn't plan on being around for much longer, as I had begun thinking about home.

We were in Winnipeg, Manitoba, one night and I was offered a tab of acid. LSD is a powerful hallucinogenic drug. Users are likely to experience a distorted view of objects and reality, including seeing and sometimes hearing things that aren't there. I would never describe myself as a drug user, but I was young and wanted to experiment, so I put the small square of blotting paper that had been soaked in the drug into my mouth. I don't remember too much about what happened after that. I have vague memories of being at a party in a magnificent house on top of a hill. I was playing slaps/knuckles with a man who must have been better than me, as my hand was all smashed up when I awoke the following morning. I can recall driving a sports car at full speed down a hill towards the hotel where the sales team and I were staying. I feel a little clearer about what happened next, but it was far from logical. I think I turned into my father. I ordered the sales team to stand in the bath in my room and I began shouting and screaming at them. They were fully clothed and terrified that I was going to harm them, but, apart from the occasional slap or lash from my belt of encouragement when I ordered them to do something, I hardly touched them.

The following day, I went out and bought a Bulova clock for my parents' forthcoming anniversary with one of my cheques. I had the clock engraved with the words, 'To the best parents in the world, happy anniversary, Wayne.' I then packed my bag and left my trembling sales team in their beds. I don't think an apology would have healed the trauma I had caused them. I took what money there was, jumped into the Volvo and drove off, hoping that I would never see them again.

I found a hotel on the other side of Winnipeg and hung around the city for a few days before becoming acquainted with a group of bikers. They invited me to a barbecue that was attended by at least 100 people, most of whom arrived on Harley-Davidson motorcycles. They spent most of the day roaring up and down the nearby lanes and dirt tracks. I had a few beers and during a conversation I mentioned that I had once been a keen boxer. One of the bikers said that Wayne Caplette, the Canadian champion, was at the barbecue. Before I knew it, I had taken my shirt off, handed over $50 and was fighting a bigger man than me who was to become the Midwest Middleweight Champion less than two years later. I gave a very good account of myself but lost. I shook hands with Caplette after the fight, got into the Volvo and returned to my hotel.

Lying on my bed that night, I decided it was time to return to Manchester. The cheques were burning a hole in my pocket, so I decided to use them up before I departed. I flew to Vancouver, where I purchased a 1978 Silver Anniversary Corvette Stingray. I gave the car salesman the Volvo in part exchange and a cheque for $23,000. Less than an hour later, I was driving through Winnipeg in my brand-new Corvette. I parked it at the hotel and went out again to buy a Bronco Blazer for $8,000. I then purchased a pack of number-seven racing stickers and put them on the Corvette. Using the cheques, I bought a self-tow trailer, shelves and boxes of snap-on tools. I then purchased return tickets on a ship bound for England for both vehicles and sent them home. Finally, I walked into a travel agency waving my last cheque and purchased a return flight from Canada to England. I cannot recall a more enjoyable trip. I was smiling when the plane took off and I was still beaming when the wheels screeched to announce our arrival at Gatwick airport.

ROUND FIVE

An Idiot Abroad

I STAYED IN a hotel at Gatwick airport for two days before moving to bed-and-breakfast accommodation in Cobham, Surrey, where I remained for six days. I then caught the train to Portsmouth harbour to await the arrival of the ship carrying the cars and trailer full of tools that I had acquired in Canada. On the day the ship docked, I presented myself at the customs desk and asked for my vehicles to be cleared.

'What is the purpose of importing these vehicles, sir?' a bored-looking officer asked.

'I live in Canada. I'm on vacation and am going to be doing some rallying. I will be returning home in six weeks. Here are the return tickets.'

I think the customs officer was more interested in the sports page of the newspaper he'd been reading because he barely glanced at the stack of paperwork I offered him. 'That's fine, sir. Enjoy your trip,' he said nonchalantly as he stamped the vehicles' documentation. I drove the Bronco out of the dock with the Corvette on the trailer and made my way to Manchester.

I had not told anybody that I was back in the country. I had been away for the best part of a year and couldn't wait to see my parents. When I pulled up outside my home I beeped the horn of the Bronco repeatedly. The lounge curtain twitched and my mother came running into the street. My father followed, scratching his head. I was bombarded with questions about my travels before we all went inside, where I gave my parents their present. I was, of course, economical with the truth when asked how I had managed to afford two vehicles and a trailer full of brand-new tools. When I said that I had worked hard and saved, there were a few raised eyebrows and smirks. I'm not sure anybody actually cared about the truth; they were just so pleased that I was home.

Within a week, I had sold both of the vehicles to Peter Wrigley, who had flown to Canada with me but returned home early. I then invested some of my ill-gotten gains in a brand-new Ford pick-up truck, which I used to earn a living sourcing and selling scrap metal.

I had not kept myself in shape while in Canada, so I returned to the gym, where I worked extremely hard. On 17 September 1979, I fought my first professional bout, against a man from Swansea named Jeff Aspell. The fight, which was held at the Piccadilly Hotel in Manchester, was over six rounds and I won on points. Less than a month later at the same venue I fought a man from Sheffield named Jimmy Ellis. The fight was again over six rounds and again I won on points. In fairness to Ellis, I do not believe that I deserved to be declared the winner. It happens a lot in boxing, the fighter from the town or city where the bout is being held is usually given the decision, unless of course he takes a blatant beating. It is generally known as 'home-boy advantage'. Eight days later, I travelled to Blackpool to fight a man named Tommy Baldwin, from Gateshead, whom I knocked out after just three rounds.

Four days later, my manager Nat Basso rang me and said, 'I've got another fight for you, kid.'

'It's a bit sudden, but no problem – I will be there,' I replied.

Nat told me that the fight was to be held in Barnsley and my opponent was a man from Nottingham named Joey Sanders. I beat Sanders on points, but he was of the opinion that he had won and immediately demanded a rematch. If I think a man has outboxed me I will say so; there is no shame in conceding you have lost a sporting contest. I had beaten Sanders and knew that if he fought me every day for the rest of his life he wouldn't win, so I accepted his challenge and less than three weeks later we fought again. The fight was held at Caister-on-Sea in Norfolk and was billed as the main event. It was the first time that I had been asked to box eight rounds, but I was confident that I could do so, as I was extremely fit and mentally focused. I knocked Sanders out with a left hook in the fourth round. As I stood back watching the referee count, I can remember thinking to myself, 'Fucking hell, I didn't even hit him properly.' Regardless of the power or otherwise of my punch, Sanders stayed down and I was paid the £250 winner's fee.

My sister was attending college around this time. Her best friend was a beautiful girl named Renee, who would occasionally visit our house. It wasn't long before I had become totally smitten. Four days after the Sanders fight I had arranged to go to a boxing show in Stockport, and so I asked Renee if she would like to come with me. I was over the moon when she accepted my invitation.

I spent the day collecting scrap metal and when I had finished I went into Nicky the Greek's barber shop on Cheatham Hill Road as I wanted to look my best for Renee. While I was sitting in the chair, the phone rang and Nicky answered it. 'It's for you, Wayne. It's your father,' he said. My father had frequented Nicky the Greek's shop for more than 20 years, so receiving business or personal calls there was not uncommon. When I asked my father what he wanted, he said that I had to ring Nat Basso straight away. There were no mobile phones in those days, so I asked Nicky if I could use his phone. When I got through to Nat, he asked me if I wanted to fight that night.

'I'm supposed to be taking a girl to a boxing show in Stockport,' I said.

'Well, that's OK. You can still both go because this fight's in Stockport – but she'll have to stay out of the ring,' Nat replied.

When I agreed to take the fight, I was told that the bout would be over eight rounds and my opponent was a Liverpudlian named Chris Glover. This guy was no mug; his last fight had been for the Central Area welterweight title. I could have done with time to train for this fight, but I was told I had to be in the ring in less than three hours because Glover's opponent had withdrawn at short notice.

When Nicky had finished cutting my hair, I jumped in my truck, drove home and prepared myself and my kit for the bout. I telephoned Renee and explained what had happened. 'I have given my sister two tickets, so you can still come and watch me. We can always go out for a drink afterwards,' I said. Renee sighed and initially declined my offer, but I somehow managed to talk her around.

Later that night, as I entered the ring, I scoured the crowd in search of Renee. It didn't take me long to find her. I raised my hand as if to wave and she smiled back at me. They could have put Mike Tyson in the ring with me that night and I would have won. Nobody was going to prevent me from impressing that vision of beauty. I defeated Glover on points and in doing so won the heart of Renee. For two glorious months, Renee and I were inseparable. Sadly, when my reputation became known to her parents they banned her from seeing me. We tried hard to meet regularly in secret, but the deception took its toll on Renee and reluctantly we parted. I often wonder what became of her and what might have been if her parents had not been so judgemental.

On 27 November 1979, I fought Jimmy Ellis in his home town of Sheffield. Ellis was still smarting from his earlier defeat by me. I was the only man ever to have beaten him, and he wanted to address that blemish on his career in front of his home crowd, friends and family. I could understand his confidence as he bounced around the ring before the fight. The crowd were chanting his name and he was boasting that he would be victorious. I say that I could understand his confidence because anybody who had watched me fight could be forgiven for thinking that I was an unskilled boxer. I would constantly move forward and appeared awkward rather than slick. It was a style that I deliberately emphasised because it made me a very difficult opponent to beat, as Ellis was soon to discover. Over eight three-minute rounds, I beat him convincingly, more so than in our first encounter.

Chris Glover, another former opponent whom I had defeated, also believed that he could beat me, so I agreed to a second bout with him. Less than two weeks after the Ellis bout I fought Glover at the Piccadilly Hotel in Manchester and won on points.

I had been fighting on an almost weekly basis for some months, and I decided to take a break over the Christmas holiday. My body benefited from this period of rest and recuperation, but my mind was forever eager to return to the ring. Although I had only taken a two-week break, I missed the excitement and thrill of being in the ring. On 7 January 1980, I fought Terry Matthews from Swansea at the Piccadilly Hotel in Manchester. The fight was over eight rounds, and, not wanting to take anything away from my opponent, I wasn't as sharp as I had been, and as I went to throw a right-hander he caught me with a left-hook sucker punch and I went down. I bounced back onto my feet at the count of three. I was in a bit of a haze, but I managed to hang on until the bell rang. I can recall my trainer Kenny Daniels saying, 'You have to win this round, Wayne. It's the last round and he is ahead of you on points.' I managed to clear my head and unleash a barrage of blows that earned me a draw. I am an honourable man, so I do not mind admitting that it was a decision that should have been given to Terry Matthews.

I spent the next two weeks training hard for my next fight, which was against a Jamaican from Wolverhampton named Dennis Pryce. The fight was held at the Great International Sporting Club in Nottingham and was over eight rounds. Pryce moved around the ring so swiftly I don't think I managed to hit him for the first three rounds. When I did succeed in cornering him, he covered up, and so the bout proved to be a rather unspectacular event. I was declared the winner.

Shortly after the Pryce fight, I fell out with my father. I cannot recall what the dispute was about, but it escalated out of all proportion and the end result was that I ended up moving to Digbeth in Birmingham. I knew a lot of people in the city because I used to sell a lot of the scrap metal I acquired in Manchester there. I don't know why, but scrap merchants would always pay top rates for metal in Birmingham. If I was offered £600 for a load of scrap in Manchester, I knew I could get £750 or more for it in Birmingham. Perhaps it was because the Midlands was the home of industry back in those days.

There was a 24-hour café near Digbeth police station where I used to buy and sell contraband. When I walked out of the café one evening, two undercover police officers informed me that I was under arrest on suspicion of handling stolen goods. When the officers searched my car, they found all the evidence they needed. The boot was an Aladdin's cave of counterfeit goods and other items that I had acquired illegally. I was subsequently charged and remanded in custody to Brockhill Young Offenders Institution in Worcestershire to await trial. I didn't relish the thought of spending the best part of a year behind bars awaiting trial for a bit of hooky merchandise, so I swallowed my pride and rang my father.

The following day, he arrived in Worcestershire and shortly afterwards I had been granted bail. On the journey home, I was lectured about the promising boxing career I was in danger of jeopardising. I was told that if I wished to waste my life languishing in jail I shouldn't have telephoned home and asked my father to arrange bail. On the other hand, if I wanted to box I now had to train hard and prove not only to my father but also to myself that boxing was my future. That evening I moved back in with my parents and thereafter spent every available hour in the gym getting myself back into shape. When I eventually appeared in court for sentencing, I was given a suspended term of imprisonment for a variety of offences relating to stolen and counterfeit goods.

On 12 May 1980, I fought at the Piccadilly Hotel in Manchester. My opponent was a man named Leo Mulhearn, who came from Doncaster. He was a tricky fighter and after four rounds I began to feel frustrated. This allowed Mulhearn to get inside and punish me with a flurry of head shots. In the seventh and eighth rounds, though, I moved around the ring snapping his head back with some beautiful jabs. I wasn't surprised, therefore, when the judges announced that I had won the bout on points.

That same week I read in the *Boxing News* magazine that a fighter named Jimmy Batten was to take on a man named Jimmy Ellis, whom I had fought and defeated on two occasions. Batten was a former British light middleweight champion who had recently lost his title at Wembley. If Ellis were to defeat Batten, he would inevitably be given the chance of a title fight, something all boxers dream of having. Young and naive about the workings of the boxing world, I took great offence that I appeared to have been overlooked for a man I had beaten twice. I phoned Nat Basso and ranted, 'I'm not standing for this liberty! What's happening here?' I am undefeated, I beat Ellis twice, I can do this and I can do that. When my tirade had subsided, Nat replied, 'You're not ready for Batten yet.' Arrogant? Guilty. Obnoxious? Guilty. Hotheaded? Guilty. I genuinely believed at that time that I could defeat any man, and I would not let up until Nat agreed to complain bitterly to the Boxing Board of Control so that I, rather than Ellis, could fight Batten.

The fight was eventually arranged for 3 June 1980 at the Royal Albert Hall in London. The pre-fight weigh-in was held at the White Horse near Shaftesbury Avenue. I was an ounce overweight, so I had to skip and run up and down the busy street until I lost the excess weight. Terry Downes, the former middleweight world champion, attended the weigh-in and had parked his Rolls-Royce outside the hotel. I noticed the vehicle when I set off on my run, but it was gone when I returned. In its place was a police vehicle and two officers were talking to Downes. I walked over and asked if everything was OK. Ignoring me, one of the officers said, 'I am sorry, Mr Downes, your vehicle was illegally parked, so we have had it towed away.' Straight-faced, Downes looked at the officer and replied, 'That's all right, son. Don't worry about it. I've got another one at home.' Downes and I then walked into the hotel, where I laughed all the way through the weigh-in.

Shortly afterwards, I went to the Regent Palace Hotel at Piccadilly Circus to prepare for the fight. With the benefit of hindsight, I should have listened to Nat Basso. I should never have fought Batten. At that time, he simply had too much experience under his belt for me. This was my 12th professional fight and Batten's 34th. I was simply not ready for such a seasoned fighter.

In the second round, I landed an absolute peach of a right-hander and Batten fell against the ropes. Here my inexperience showed. I moved in for what I thought would be the kill, but Batten used his head to break my nose. As I stepped back, blood poured down my face and chest. I can remember thinking, 'You dirty so and so. I wish I would have thought of doing that.' It wasn't dirty, though; Jimmy Batten was a professional fighter doing things that I was yet to learn.

By the end of the third round, my eyes were so swollen I could hardly see. I only knew one way to fight and that was to keep going forward, but every time I took a step in Batten's direction he would punish me. While trying to patch me up, my trainer, Kenny Daniels, said to me, 'It's not your night, son. Do you want me to pull you out?'

'I have got eight rounds to get through,' I replied. 'If you do try to pull me out, I will knock you out.'

I thought I improved considerably in the fourth round. I was working Batten out and managing to hit him with a few decent punches. Then, midway through that round, Batten hit me with a left uppercut that I did not see until later that night on the television replays. All I remember is his fist striking me in the solar plexus and a gush of air rapidly exiting via my mouth. I couldn't breathe in and was forced to drop down on one knee. Larry O'Connell, the referee, looked down at me and signalled the end of the fight.

I personally thought I could have fought on, but then I have to concede that I had also truly believed that I could defeat Jimmy Batten. Self-belief is a great asset to a boxer, but if any young fighters are reading this my advice is at least listen to your trainer. Not long after fighting me, Jimmy Batten fought Roberto Durán, arguably one of the greatest boxers of all time. In 103 professional fights, Durán knocked out 70 of his opponents. Batten fought Durán in Miami over ten rounds and, after giving a good account of himself, lost the bout on points – proof if any were needed that Batten was no mug.

I returned to Manchester disillusioned and with my tail firmly between my legs. My first defeat in professional boxing had a profound effect upon me. I began to wonder if I would be better off fighting men for money rather than training for weeks to take them on for belts and titles.

I met a rugby player whom I shall call Peter. His father owned a large and successful haulage company in Salford. Like me, Peter lived his life under the very watchful eye of his father. We therefore had some of the same gripes about life and not surprisingly we got on well. Peter told me that his father's vehicles were used to export car engines to Malta. Never one to miss an opportunity, I did a little research and soon discovered that the most sought-after engines in Malta could be found in BMC 550 FG trucks and in the licensed taxis that were used throughout Manchester.

One night I dispatched a group of lads to Moore's Bakery on Fitzwarren Street in Salford. There they stole all 26 BMC 550 FG trucks that the bakery owned. The vehicles were driven to a yard, dismantled within two days, boxed up and exported to Malta. The trucks' aluminium box bodies were cut up and sold as scrap.

Over the next few months, car thieves were stealing every taxi and truck that they could lay their hands on for me. The Maltese were soon on the phone demanding generators, dumper trucks and any other sort of machinery that I could source. When the vehicles and parts arrived in Malta, my money would be transferred into a bank account before they were unloaded. I would then receive a phone call and arrange to pick up the cash from Peter's father's yard.

One day I was in the company of a car thief when I received a call to go and collect £7,000. As we entered the industrial estate where Peter's father's yard was, the car thief began shouting, 'Filth, filth, filth!' The next thing I knew he had opened the car door and launched himself out onto the street. I hadn't even had time to slow down. When I looked around, I could see four police cars parked adjacent to Peter's father's business premises. I continued driving into the yard, parked and walked up a set of stairs into a Portakabin. As I entered, I could see Peter and his father sat at a desk and two men in suits sitting opposite them.

'Have you got my money?' I asked Peter.

'These men wish to speak to you,' he replied, looking at the officers.

Ignoring his response completely, I glared at Peter. 'I have just asked you a fucking question. Have you got my money?'

Peter looked at me, opened a drawer and handed me a bulging brown A4-sized envelope.

I snatched the envelope and turned to gaze at the two policemen. 'And who are you?' I snarled.

Mumbling, one of the officers replied, 'We are from the Crescent Police Station and, erm . . . we need to talk to you.'

Cutting him short, I shouted, 'If you want to talk to me, contact my fucking solicitor.' I then stormed out, slamming the door behind me.

I couldn't help but laugh as I drove away, because I could see the two confused officers scratching their heads outside the Portakabin in my rear-view mirror. My 'in their face' attitude had undoubtedly disassembled any strategy that they had planned before my arrival.

When I arrived home, my father asked me what time I

was going to the gym for training, but I informed him that I wasn't going anywhere that night. The windows of our lounge overlooked the street. Every time I heard a vehicle approaching, I would jump up to see if it was the police. My father kept asking me what was wrong, but I denied that there was a problem. At approximately 7.30 p.m., I heard the roar of engines and looked out into the street to see a fleet of police cars and vans pulling up outside the house. Without saying a word, I walked into the kitchen, opened the back door and ran.

I wasn't sure what I should do, but I went to the home of a lad named Tony, who often supplied me with stolen property. After discussing my predicament, we agreed that the most sensible option would be for me to leave Manchester for a while. Tony gave me a lift to the Ordsall district of the city, assuring me that a friend of his named Jimmy would be able to fix me up with a car. When we arrived at Jimmy's, I could see six vehicles parked on and around his drive, all of which, I later learned, were stolen. After Terry had introduced me to Jimmy, I said that I not only needed a car but also somebody to drive me to London, for which I would pay cash. Jimmy suggested that I buy a brand-new Ford Fiesta Supersport that he had stolen; he was also willing to drive for me. I shook Jimmy's hand, gave him a wad of money and said that I wanted to leave immediately.

When we arrived in the capital, I booked two rooms at the Regent Palace Hotel, where I had stayed prior to fighting Jimmy Batten. The following morning, I took my new friend Jimmy to meet Johnny Waldron, whom I had fought and defeated twice on Epsom Downs. Jimmy and I ended up spending three days at Johnny's home before deciding to travel over to France.

There was no master plan; we were just going to arrive and see which way the wind would blow us. Because our vehicle was stolen, we decided to leave it in Dover and acquire a replacement when we arrived in Calais. Before the anchor of our ferry had settled on the seabed in France, Jimmy was screeching up alongside me in a brand-new Citroën. We loaded up our luggage and drove to a local hotel, where we spent the night with two French girls we met in a bar. The following morning, Jimmy and I headed for Paris.

Neither of us had been before, so we decided to park the Citroën near a landmark to make it easier to find. I noticed a Kickers shop and naively suggested that there could only be one in Paris so we should park there. (I wasn't aware that Kickers footwear was in fact made in France.) We spent all day and a substantial part of the evening sightseeing before returning to where we thought we had parked the car. We were outside a Kickers shop, but there was no sign of the vehicle, so we asked a local if there was another store nearby. After finding at least six Kickers shops but no stolen Citroën, we agreed that Jimmy would acquire another vehicle.

That night, we drove for nearly nine hours to the coastal resort of Cannes. We slept for a couple of hours in the car and then drove to the entrance of the exclusive Carlton Hotel, which overlooks the Mediterranean. As you enter the hotel, there is a ramp that leads down to an underground car park. Jimmy manoeuvred our stolen vehicle down the ramp and as we turned a bend we were forced to stop in front of a large steel shutter. Jimmy's initial reaction was to reverse, but when he looked in his rear-view mirror he saw a Rolls-Royce just inches from our bumper. When I saw the Rolls-Royce, I said to Jimmy, 'Get out and tell that arsehole to back up as we need to get out of here.' I stared at the rear-view mirror as Jimmy approached the passenger side of the vehicle. I had no idea what he had said, but when he returned to our vehicle he was laughing.

'What's so funny?' I asked as Jimmy reversed back up the ramp at speed.

'When I leaned in the car to talk to the guy, I grabbed this without him noticing,' Jimmy replied as he tossed a large money belt into my lap.

The belt contained several hundred French francs and vehicle documentation for the Rolls-Royce and a Mercedes SL. I told Jimmy that I wanted him to steal the vehicles so that we could take them back to England, where we could sell them as we were in possession of all the relevant paperwork. I retreated to a nearby café for lunch while Jimmy returned to the car park to take the first of the two vehicles. I nearly choked on my omelette with laughter when I saw Jimmy, a young street urchin from Manchester, driving out of the Carlton Hotel car park behind the wheel of a brand-new Rolls-Royce. 'Park that up near our car and go back for the Mercedes SL,' I told Jimmy as he pulled up outside the café. I watched as Jimmy once more disappeared down the ramp into the hotel car park.

When an hour had passed I just knew that he had been caught, although there was always the possibility that the Mercedes SL was not there or wouldn't start. I decided that I would walk down to the car park to see if there was any police activity. Apart from one or two hotel customers dragging suitcases to and from their cars, I couldn't see anybody. I did notice a pile of broken glass in an empty parking space and I assumed that Jimmy had broken a window to gain entry to the Rolls-Royce. I walked back out into the street and looked around, but there was no sign of Jimmy or the Mercedes SL.

The little man whom I then noticed walking towards me instantly reminded me of Fred Flintstone, the cartoon character. I thought that he might have realised that I was smirking at the resemblance, because he started barking orders at me in French. 'English, English, no understand,' I replied. The next thing I knew I was buried beneath five or six police officers and a white Transit-type van had screeched to a halt at the kerbside. A sliding side door opened and I was bundled into a seat behind Jimmy.

I can only describe the police station as open plan with a Wild West theme. There was a large cage in the corner of the main office; its bars were embedded in both the ceiling and floor. Approximately eight prisoners were being held in this 'cell', which was about seven metres long and four metres wide. One of the prisoners was an African who was clearly either drunk, drugged or both. He greeted me and Jimmy and asked if there was anything we needed. 'I could do with a drink. I'm parched,' I replied. To my surprise, he handed over a bottle of beer and assured me that there was more if I wanted it.

The following morning, Jimmy and I appeared in court hungover and were sentenced to serve six months' imprisonment. We were then taken to Grasse prison, which is perched on top of a mountain on the outskirts of Cannes. Twice a day we were allowed to spend two hours in a courtyard for what the French called *promenade*. Four large steel cages contained the inmates in the yard and these were monitored by armed guards who stood above them on walkways. Promenade was supposed to be an exercise period, but most of the Caucasian prisoners spent the two-hour period basking in the sunshine. One or two of the inmates tried to make conversation, but I couldn't understand them and preferred to concentrate on my suntan.

Hands up, I was possibly being ignorant, but more likely I couldn't be arsed; whatever my reason, I didn't even attempt to learn French. Jimmy, on the other hand, tried hard to communicate with our captors and before long he was chatting away to them in their native tongue. 'You ought to be careful with your blonde hair, blue eyes and soft French accent. Somebody will want you as their bitch, Jimmy,' I warned him. Jimmy laughed, but I wasn't sure that some of the long-term prisoners hadn't already made plans involving him and their lack of sexual activity. When a Moroccan with no teeth and less manners attempted to grab Jimmy, I knocked him out with one punch and was dragged off to the punishment block.

Grasse's punishment block was exactly what it said on the tin. My bed was made of stone, my pillow was made of stone and my toilet was made of stone. 'Food' for want of a better word, amounted to a stone bowl of dirty water with a few twigs sprinkled on the top. The hot Mediterranean sun turned my stone tomb into an oven during the day and a fucking fridge freezer at night. After two weeks, I was taken back to my cell in the main prison.

The other inmates gave me a wide berth after witnessing what had happened to the Moroccan, so Jimmy and I were permitted to serve out the remainder of our sentences in relative peace. On the day of our release, we were given a 60-franc discharge grant, which we used to purchase train tickets to Nice. We had spent our meagre grant, so I told Jimmy that he would have to acquire a car for us, which he quickly did. We then spent the next few days driving around the south of France breaking into cars and stealing anything of value that we could lay our hands on.

In Marseilles, Jimmy crept into the back of an Algerian café and stole the takings from the till. Unfortunately for him and me, the owner spotted him and gave chase. I was waiting for him in a stolen car parked in a small square surrounded by shops. As he came running towards me, I jumped out of the vehicle and picked up a chair to fend off the irate Algerian café proprietor. He pulled out a knife and within seconds had been joined by several other angry-looking Algerians. Jimmy and I launched chair after chair at the mob as we retreated from the square, but they kept advancing on us. We eventually decided it would be safer simply to run. We dashed to the railway station, where we managed to board a train for Paris.

When we arrived in the French capital, we walked out of the station and Jimmy immediately stole another vehicle, as we had decided to catch the ferry home. Later that night, we arrived at the port of Dieppe without a franc between us. All of our money and personal effects had been left in the stolen vehicle in Marseilles. I approached a group of tall, heavily built Dutchmen who were on the quayside and said in pidgin English, 'You fight? You fight with me? We put money down and winner keeps, yes?' It's not the type of money-making scheme that would curry favour with the likes of Lord Alan Sugar, but it was the only idea I had that night. Fortunately, one of the Dutchmen agreed to fight me for 100 francs. Unfortunately, he happened to be the biggest man in the group. We walked to a car park, took off our shirts and the fight began. I kept my distance from my opponent but still managed to land punch after punch until he had weakened. Eventually, I moved in and delivered a combination of blows that sent him crashing to the ground. Respect where it's due, the man got up, shook my hand and handed over 100 francs. I had been confident that I would win, not because I was in particularly good shape – I wasn't – I just couldn't contemplate defeat because I didn't have the money to pay my opponent.

As we sat talking to the Dutchmen, I had another idea that I thought might swell our coffers. 'I am taking bets on how long it will take for our car to sink in this harbour,' I said. The Dutchmen all laughed, but I told them that I was deadly serious. They all placed a bet before Jimmy and I pushed the stolen car off the harbour and into the sea. The vehicle floated for what seemed an eternity before the waves smashed it against the harbour wall and it sank bonnet first. Jimmy and I lost a large portion of the winnings I had secured in the car-park brawl, but we still had enough to purchase tickets for the ferry.

As we attempted to board the vessel, we were stopped by immigration officers. We didn't have any personal possessions or passports, so we had to explain that we had lost them. One of the officers took photographs of Jimmy and me, and asked us to fill out forms that he said would secure our passage home. Dieppe to Newhaven is a long crossing and the sea that night was particularly rough, so Jimmy and I went to sleep on chairs in a designated quiet zone.

When the ferry docked in England, we were the first passengers to go through passport control and customs. I had noticed the ship's purser heading towards the immigration office with our forms and so had power-walked Jimmy off the boat. I had no doubt the police in Salford still wanted to talk to me about the stolen goods that had been exported to Malta, so I didn't want customs or any other authority scrutinising me.

As we walked out of the terminal there was an empty taxi at the roadside with its engine still running.

'Shall we take a taxi, Jimmy?' I asked, pointing towards the vehicle.

'No, let's just walk up the road. We'll get a car there,' Jimmy replied.

Moments later, we were surrounded by police officers who informed us that we were under arrest.

Within a short period of time, Jimmy had been released without charge, but I was kept in Newhaven police station for three days while Salford police arranged for two detectives to come and collect me. Prior to their arrival, I had spoken to my father on the phone and he had subsequently given my solicitor a wad of receipts for engines that I had supposedly purchased. Later, during interview at the Crescent Police Station in Salford, I produced the receipts, but the officers knew that they were not genuine and charged me with theft and handling stolen goods.

When I appeared in court the police opposed bail because they said they believed that I would once more flee the country. Despite a strong argument being delivered eloquently by my solicitor, the magistrate agreed with the police and I was remanded in custody to HMP Strangeways to await trial.

ROUND SIX

The Strangeways Hotel

THE NAME WAYNE Barker was replaced by a number: M96547. I was then housed in cell number 14 on landing E2. The view wasn't great, but the facilities slightly edged my tombstone abode back in Grasse prison. I had been in custody several times before, but this was my first real taste of a British prison. In my home town and surrounded by others who shared my native tongue, it actually felt like I had lost my liberty. In comparison, Grasse had been little more than a holiday home, albeit from hell.

I don't care for bad manners and poor personal hygiene, so I found it hard to share my cell with any of the reprobates that the prison staff deposited at my door. Most took my refusal to let them enter well; one or two took offence and we ended up exchanging blows. Eventually, the prison officers gave up trying to make me share my meagre space and I was generally permitted to enjoy it alone.

However, Strangeways was notorious for its overcrowded conditions, so when the city's magistrates were feeling less than merciful the jail would end up bursting at the seams. During one such week, I returned from a visit to find the name card of a prisoner adjacent to mine on the cell door. 'Pack your gear, mate. You've got to move,' I said as I entered the cell. A man in his early 20s was sitting on the lower bunk. He looked up and asked what I meant.

'No offence. Nothing personal. You just have to pack your stuff and leave this cell now,' I replied.

'You can't talk to me like that and you wouldn't if you knew what I was in for,' the man said.

I asked him what crime he had committed to be banished to this godforsaken place and added that regardless of his alleged misdemeanour I could and would talk to him as I saw fit.

'I've murdered somebody,' the man said.

'And who would that be?' I enquired.

'A nigger. I stabbed him after a dispute in Fallowfield,' the man said with a smirk.

I struggled to contain my anger because I knew the answer to the next question that I was about to ask. Only one non-white person had been murdered in the Fallowfield district of Manchester that week as far as I knew. He was a 14-year-old boy named Louston Pantry and I knew his family personally.

'So who is this nigger you murdered?' I asked as I prepared to unleash my anger.

'Louston Pantry. He was throwing things at a car I was in and he paid the price,' he replied.

I knew Louston's elder brother Seymour very well. I had bounced Louston on my knee many a time while his mother, Joyce, prepared a meal for me. The family were good, decent people, and here I was about to be locked in a cell with a fucking animal that was gloating over murdering one of them. Instead of exploding into a violent rage, my mind and body automatically slipped into an almost robotic state. I subconsciously knew that this situation was going to develop into something extremely serious; I was calm and knew exactly what I had to do.

I listened as if interested as the animal explained how Louston was one of a group of eight children who had been picking pears from an orchard. The fruit was so bitter it was inedible, so two of the boys began hurling it at passing cars. One of those cars was occupied by the man in my cell, Stephen Whittington, and his 29-year-old friend Joseph Moreton. 'They nearly broke the fucking windscreen, so we decided to teach the little bastards a lesson,' my cell-mate said. He explained that their car had stopped and he and his friend had got out. 'The bastards ran away, but we chased them and caught one of them. We both held him and I stabbed him.'

I knew the rest of the grisly story because I had read about the incident in the local newspaper. The men had chased the 14-year-old child shouting, 'Come here, you black bastard.' Louston tried in vain to escape. When they caught him, Moreton and Whittington held Louston's arms and Whittington stabbed the child in the abdomen with a sheath knife. The blade penetrated Louston's stomach and almost severed his spine. The cowards then ran away. Drenched in his own blood, Louston staggered to the garden wall of a nearby vicarage, somehow managed to climb it and then collapsed. The vicar was tending his garden and when he saw Louston lying at the foot of his wall he ran to his aid. Sadly, the boy died in hospital several hours later.

While we had been talking, a prison officer had walked along the landing locking all of the cell doors. I couldn't now throw my unwanted guest out, so I pretended that the frosty exterior I had initially presented him with had now thawed. At 4.30 p.m. the cell door was unlocked so that we could go down to the servery for our evening meal. As I went to leave my cell, I was confronted by a group of inmates who were trying to enter.

'What's going on? What's the problem?' I asked.

'Stephen Whittington, that fucking nonce in your cell. We're going to do him,' one of the men replied.

I told them that any attack on a man in my cell was not going to happen; I would deal with matters.

I asked Whittington if he was coming to fetch his meal, but the hard man appeared to have lost his appetite as well as his bravado. I slammed the cell door, locking Whittington safely inside, and went off to collect my food.

When I returned to the cell, I did my best to make Whittington feel at ease. I told him, 'If someone is going to do something in here, they won't warn you. They'll just do it. Those people who came to the door are all talk.' At 6 p.m., the cell doors were unlocked so that inmates could put their used meal trays out, go to the toilet and get fresh water. Whittington still refused to leave the cell. We were then locked up for the night. At 7.30 p.m., a tea urn was wheeled along the landing and each inmate was given a cup of tea and a bun. After that, the prison staff did a headcount and we were not disturbed again until the morning.

As soon as the prison landing fell silent, I began pacing the cell. Whittington was terrified and sat on the lower bunk looking extremely nervous. After a few minutes, I slapped him hard across the face with the back of my hand. 'So you like killing little nigger boys, do you? That little nigger, as you call him, was a personal friend of mine,' I said. The colour drained from Whittington's face. He knew that his punishment had only just begun and he was terror-stricken. He had every reason to be so. Throughout that evening, I systematically tortured and beat Whittington. I want to say here and now that I am not bragging about this incident, nor am I proud of it, but I have no regrets. It is an event that happened and affected my future, and as this is my life story it needs to be told.

After punching Whittington into submission, I bound his

hands and feet and gagged him to muffle any screams. Using a razor blade, I cut around the soles of his feet and then pulled off all of the skin covering the bottom of his feet. As I ripped the thick skin from his flesh, Whittington struggled violently before passing out with pain. I revived him by stubbing numerous cigarettes out all over his body, being careful not to cause injury where anybody would see. After removing his upper clothing, I cut deep gorges into his chest, stomach and back. On his arms, I played noughts and crosses using the blood-soaked razor blade. Whittington was barely conscious and his body was producing a kind of thick, oily, cold sweat. I am not a medical man, but I guessed that he was in deep shock and so I gave him breaks in between each punishment.

At 4 a.m., I decided that I would have to clean Whittington up before the prison staff opened the door. I had two hours, but with the state Whittington was in I was still going to have to rush. I cut our bed-sheets up and began wrapping makeshift bandages around his feet, legs, arms and torso. His feet were the most difficult to treat. They resembled two lumps of raw meat and were horribly swollen. I decided to lay Whittington in his bed and tell the prison staff that he was unwell. That would give his feet a few days to begin to heal and nobody would notice his wounds. I very much doubted that he would be able to walk in any event, so bed was undoubtedly his and my best option.

'If you utter one fucking word about this, you will be joining your fucking victim,' I warned Whittington just before our door was unlocked.

'I won't, I promise I won't, just don't hurt me, please don't hurt me,' he replied.

When our cell door was opened, I told the prison officer that Whittington had endured a bad night. 'He is ill. It must have been something he ate,' I added. Glancing around the door at Whittington, the officer said, 'Bloody hell, you do look rough Whittington. Stay where you are and if you get any worse I'll call the doctor.'

Over the next few days, I was on edge. I thought Whittington might tell the prison staff what I had done, but surprisingly he kept his mouth shut. He did, however, move out of my cell as soon as he was able to hobble.

When Whittington eventually appeared in court, he and the driver of the vehicle, Joseph Moreton, pleaded not guilty. Several witnesses, including a local resident named John O'Brian, described seeing Moreton pull up in a Ford Capri before he and Whittington jumped out and chased a group of children. They caught Louston Pantry, held him by both arms and then Whittington plunged the blade into the child's stomach. It penetrated his spine. One of the two men then said, 'Let's get going.'

Whittington told the jury that he remembered cornering Louston but during the struggle that the young boy put up he had accidentally stabbed him. Jurors saw straight through Whittington's lies and convicted him and Moreton of murder. Whittington was sentenced to be detained at Her Majesty's pleasure (indefinitely) and Moreton was given a life sentence.

Outside the court, Mrs Pantry told reporters, 'The facts may indicate there was a racial motive because my child was the only black child in the group of eight who had been scrumping for pears. It is a bad thing to keep thinking black and white. I have no bitterness at all – except to those two people who have taken my lad from me. This shows you can get justice from British courts. I have had doubts, but I believe there was no racial motive involved.' I didn't have the heart to break the news to Mrs Pantry. If she had heard the foul-mouthed ramblings of the racist in my cell, I am in no doubt that she would have held a different view.

On 8 December 1980, I appeared at Manchester Crown

Court, where I pleaded guilty to handling stolen property. Considering the amount of money I had earned from exporting goods to Malta, I was quite pleased when the judge only sentenced me to one year in jail. Having been convicted, I was moved to another wing in Strangeways and given a job in the laundry room.

In January 1981, Whittington was asked to undergo a routine prison medical. When he took off his shirt, the doctor immediately summoned a prison officer who demanded to know how he had suffered such horrific injuries. Whittington apparently broke down and told the full story of his ordeal. Two prison officers came to my workplace later that day and said that they had to escort me to the wing office. I was informed that a serious allegation had been made against me and I was being taken to the prison gate where the police and my solicitor were waiting. 'Wayne Barker, I am arresting you for the attempted murder of Stephen Whittington,' a policeman said.

My solicitor advised me to remain calm and explained that I was going to be taken to a police station. Once there, I was interviewed about the injuries Whittington had suffered in my cell, but I refused to comment. I was subsequently charged with the attempted murder of Stephen Whittington and transferred to the prison segregation unit, which is more commonly known as 'the block'. I remained there for five months.

During visits from my father, I strenuously denied that I had touched Whittington. I told him that I was entirely innocent and was being fitted up. My father believed me simply because he had no reason to doubt me. I was nearing the end of my sentence for handling stolen goods, so my father employed a solicitor to make an application for bail at the High Court. The day before I was due to be released, the application was made, but I was not allowed to attend the hearing. I was later told that the judge had mumbled and shaken his head while reading how I had fled from Peter's father's yard and gone on the run to France after the police had arrived at my home. 'This young man even tried to flee when he got off the ferry at Newhaven. Why should I believe he won't flee again if he is granted bail in the morning?' the judge asked. My solicitor requested a brief conference with my father and when this was granted they stood in a huddle whispering to each other. Eventually, it was suggested and agreed that if my father was prepared to lodge £12,000 in cash with the court I would be granted bail. That was a lot of money back then. The average wage was just £6,000 per year, petrol cost 28 pence per litre and a pint of beer was 35 pence. Little wonder my father left the courtroom shaking his head in disbelief and bewilderment.

My mother was very good friends with the Reverend Noel Proctor, who happened to be the prison chaplain. She had telephoned Reverend Proctor and told him to tell me that I had been granted bail. When the prison staff began talking about moving me back to the remand wing the following day, I just laughed at them, as I knew that it wasn't going to happen. 'I have got bail and the only place I am going in the morning is home,' I said. The next day, the prison had still not been notified that I had been granted bail, so I sat in the wing office and refused to move until they had telephoned the court. At 11.30 a.m., the call came through and I was released from Strangeways prison but given a stark warning that I was not entirely free: I was now on bail for attempted murder.

Following my release, I heard that a trainer at Collyhurst and Moston Lads Boxing Club named Brian Hughes (now Brian Hughes MBE) had a team going to America, so I contacted Nat Basso to see if I could join them.

'Is it true that you are the secretary of the Central Area Boxing Council of the British Boxing Board of Control?' I asked.

'It is true,' Nat replied.

After pausing momentarily, I said, 'Well, can you tell me why Brian Hughes is allowed to take a squad of boxers from Manchester to America and everybody going happens to be from his club? I want to be on that team and he should be taking lads from different clubs.'

I could almost hear Nat's brain trying to work out what scam I was trying to pull. He pointed out that Brian wasn't my trainer and questioned why I would want to go to America.

'I've just come out of jail after being away in France. I haven't trained for ages and as you well know the last fight I had I lost to Jimmy Batten. I'm rusty. I need the experience,' I pleaded.

I'm not sure what strings Nat pulled, but within a day I was notified that I too would be flying out to America with Brian, who was unaware of my trouble with the police. The team consisted of four boxers: me, Peter Bassett, Eddie Smith and Ensley 'Bingo' Bingham, who went on to win the British light middleweight title.

I arrived at JFK airport in New York dressed like Mr. T from the television series *The A-Team*. Heavy gold chains adorned my neck; I wore several thick gold rings and had a large gold watch on each arm. In my suitcase, I had £10,000 in cash. After clearing immigration, we caught a flight to Detroit. I don't mind admitting it was one of the most frightening experiences of my life. The plane flew into a storm that tossed it around like a beach-ball at sea. Grown men cried as we lurched from side to side, and even a member of the cabin crew screamed out at one stage. If that particular aircraft is still in service, I guarantee impressions of my fingers will still be visible on the underside of my seat.

When we landed in Detroit, we got into a taxi and gave the driver the address of a YMCA that Brian Hughes had booked us into. I was sitting in the front of the vehicle; Brian Hughes and the other three lads were in the back. I was eyeing the meter suspiciously and when it reached $60 I asked the driver if he thought we were thick. 'We have been past this building three fucking times, mate. You're trying to rinse us,' I said. Brian Hughes jumped to the driver's defence and I began to argue with him. 'He's pulling our strides down just because we're English. How the fuck do you know where we're going, Brian? He's robbing us.' Brian was doing his best to be reasonable and I was a hotheaded young tearaway, but I would never have accepted that at that time. I therefore continued to argue with Brian and the driver until we reached our destination. The atmosphere between Brian and me wasn't very pleasant after that and that remained the case throughout the trip.

The following morning, we went to the famous Kronk Gym, which was located in the basement of an old recreation centre. The Kronk Gym earned its legendary status during the late 1970s, when boxers like Hilmer Kenty, Thomas 'The Hitman' Hearns and Mickey Goodwin trained there. In 1980, Kenty became the Kronk's first world champion and Hearns followed him just months later. The trainer was a guy called Emanuel Steward who would go on to train Wladimir Klitschko amongst others.

While at the gym, we did a bit of bag work and met a few of the local boxers. Afterwards, I was in the changing-room and an American lad came in. We began to chat.

'So how many fights have you had, man?' the American said to me.

'Twelve professional fights,' I replied.

The American laughed and said, 'Twelve fights and your nose looks like that? What hit you, man, a bus?'

I imagine he knew instantly what it was like to be hit by a bus, because he flew into the dressing-room wall. To remind him of the experience, I hit him repeatedly with left and right uppercuts and hooks. When they heard the ear-piercing screams for help, boxers from the gym swarmed into the dressing-room and leapt on top of me. 'No more, man, no more! He's had enough!' they shouted as they attempted to restrain me.

Ten minutes later, Brian Hughes led me and the other lads out of the gym with his head bowed. 'You have let the team down, Wayne,' Brian mumbled. I had been insulted and had reacted in the only way I knew how. I failed to see how that had let anybody down. When the others got in a taxi to return to the YMCA, I said that I was going for a walk. I had no idea where I was heading. I just wanted to be alone.

As I was walking down the street, I noticed a Cadillac Brougham Sedan for sale on a car lot for $550. I walked into the office, gave the guy $500 and ten minutes later I was pulling up in it outside the YMCA. I beeped the horn until the other lads came out, with Brian Hughes in tow.

'Where have you got that car from lad? Have you stolen it?' Brian asked, with a growing sense of despair.

'Of course I haven't. I bought it. Jump in, lads,' I replied.

Although I was roughly the same age as the other lads, I don't think they were as worldly as me. When I had been in Ireland fighting grown men for a few pounds, they had still been colouring in pictures at school. Rather than getting into the car for an exciting drive around Detroit city, they bowed their heads and walked meekly behind Brian back into the YMCA.

After that incident, I didn't bother inviting the other lads anywhere. I ended up doing my own thing during the spare time we had, although I still attended the gym with them. I have to admit that being in Detroit was a fantastic experience. I sparred with the likes of Tommy Hearns, whom I confess I couldn't even get near to in the ring. I also sparred with William 'Caveman' Lee, who went on to fight Marvin Hagler for the world middleweight title. When that session started, Lee headed straight for me and knocked me down with his first punch. As soon as I hit the canvas, I felt myself being dragged through the ropes by my feet.

'What's going on? I didn't even get a chance to hit him,' I said.

'When you get put down, the show's over. You'll have to wait your turn to try again,' the trainer explained.

I waited all day, but the queue of lads in front of me meant that my one and only chance had passed. This was the American way; the brightest prospects in the gym were given a never-ending line of sparring partners. Each would present a different style of boxing for the fighter to work out and defeat. The fighter's ability to box different styles would be enhanced and the kids sparring were being given the experience of taking on a world-class fighter.

I couldn't argue with the way they trained. Using just a couple of punchbags and a boxing ring, the people at the Kronk Gym had produced world champions. I had always imagined that the Americans had the best gyms in the world, but it turned out that people here in the UK have better gyms in their garages. It was all about their training regimes and ethics, I learned. That was what made their boxers some of the best in the world.

While driving around Detroit, I had noticed a nightclub called Park Lane and decided that I would go there that night. After getting suited and booted, I bade the rest of our boxing team goodnight and jumped into my Cadillac. As I walked into the Park Lane club, I became a little apprehensive. The place looked sensational, but I was the only white man in there. My sixth sense told me that I should leave, but I wasn't the type to run from trouble. I ordered a Bacardi and Coke and sat at the bar. As I ordered my third drink, I noticed a monster of a man glaring across the room at me. His nose, which spanned the width of his face, indicated that he had probably had a few fights. Sipping my drink, I prepared to leap to my feet as he came stomping towards me. 'Aren't you one of those English dudes that are training at our gym?' he said as he reached me. A sense of relief swept over me. I just hoped that he wasn't friends with the guy who had joked about my nose. 'William Lee, but most folks around here call me Caveman,' he said as he extended his hand for me to shake. I hadn't spent very long in his company in the ring, so it was perfectly reasonable that I hadn't recognised him.

William invited me to sit with him and his friends, and as I was alone I accepted. That night was one of the most memorable of my life. William and his friends took me around the clubs in Detroit and introduced me to a whole host of useful and interesting people. I was saddened to read just two years later that after William had lost a world title fight against Marvin Hagler he had gone off the rails. William began using cocaine and ended up spending a total of 16 years in prison for armed robberies. William is free of drugs now, thankfully, and works with kids occasionally at the Kronk Gym.

One of the men William introduced me to was a former welterweight champion of the world. I agreed that I would meet this former champion at a gym the following day, as he said he had a proposition for me. When I arrived for the meeting, I was led into an office where four burly men were seated. It was all very hospitable. They said that if I signed a contract with them I would be given an apartment, a car and $250 pocket money each week. In return, I would train and fight when they told me. It was crystal clear to me that I was in the company of some pretty heavy villains, so rather than show disrespect I thanked them for their generous offer and promised I would think about it. I spent three days with the former champion, but it was blatantly obvious that his people wanted to control me rather than further my boxing career.

On the fourth day, I got up and drove to the car lot where I had bought the Cadillac. I told the proprietor that I was returning to England and so no longer needed the car. He agreed to buy it back from me for $350. Brian and the boxing team planned to visit a boxing manager named Jim Jacobs in New York City prior to going home, but I had grown tired of Detroit and decided to fly there in advance.

I prepared myself for a row with Brian, but when I broke the news to him he actually looked pleased. I am not going to pull any punches here, I disliked Brian with a passion and I'm sure he disliked me. We cannot get on with every person we meet in life and that is just the way it was between us. No snide comments, no disrespect, it is what it is. I told the other lads in the team that I would find them at a gym in New York and set off to catch my flight.

After arriving in New York, I began training at the then relatively new Times Square Gym and the world-famous Gleason's Gym, where fighters such as Jake LaMotta, Roberto Durán, Mike Tyson and Muhammad Ali had trained. I was keen, young, loud and English, so by the time Brian Hughes and the lads arrived I was on first-name terms with all the regulars in both establishments.

One of the reasons Brian had included New York on the team's itinerary was because Jim Jacobs and a man named Bill Cayton had amassed the world's largest collection of fight films (between 16,000 and 26,000), dating from the

1890s through to the present day. Brian wanted to obtain copies of certain fights, but when he arrived at Jacobs' office it was closed. Jim Jacobs had been the manager of two world champions, Edwin Rosario, a three-time lightweight champion, and Wilfred Benítez, a light welterweight, welterweight and light middleweight champion. Later in his career, Jacobs co-managed Mike Tyson. Jacobs was clearly a busy man, but, although he hadn't made an appointment, Brian Hughes didn't seem to understand why he had closed his office for the day.

I knew Brian and the boxing team were flying home that night, so I taunted him, saying, 'You fucking need me now, don't you? I'm not flying back to England, so I could – if I wanted – pick the films up for you tomorrow.' Forever suspicious of me and my intentions, Brian asked if I was flying home the following week. When I confirmed that I was, he handed over several hundred dollars for the films. The only films that money was ever going to be spent on were the latest blockbusters at the Times Square Odeon.

After Brian and the team had flown home, I did go to see Jim Jacobs, but it wasn't about the films. I walked into his office and offered him my hand. 'Good morning, Mr Jacobs,' I said. 'My name's Wayne Barker. I am from Salford in England and I have come to New York to fight.' Before Jacobs could reply, his phone rang. 'Excuse me one moment,' he said as he picked up the receiver. After a few seconds, Jacobs' face lit up and he began looking me up and down. I had no idea who he was talking to, but it soon became clear that he had begun talking about me. 'It's funny you should ring and say that. I have a lad here in my office who is looking for a fight,' Jacobs said to the caller. Moments later, Jacobs handed me the receiver and said, 'This guy knows you. He wants a word.'

When I asked who was on the line, the unmistakable voice

of Mickey Duff, the boxing promoter, replied, 'Hi, Wayne. What are you doing in New York?' I had met Mickey on the boxing circuit back in England and had got to know him reasonably well. I told Mickey that I had travelled to America in search of new challenges, as I had become rusty in the ring back home.

'Does Nat Basso know what you're up to?' Mickey asked.

'Not really. But forget Nat for a minute, Mickey. Tell this man here to get me a few fights,' I replied, before handing Jacobs the phone.

Following a brief conversation, Jacobs replaced the receiver and told me to get myself down to Gleason's gym, get fit, and only then would he organise a fight for me. I didn't need telling twice. I thanked Jacobs and told him that I would keep in touch.

I rented a room in a block of run-down apartments on the corner of West 43rd Street and Broadway. It was near glitzy Times Square, but the only things that shone in my room were the silverfish and the cockroaches. One of the prettiest women I have ever seen in my life lived in the same block. Kay not only had a supermodel face, she had the body to match. Because I was English, she paid me more attention than I might have got otherwise. We went out a few times together and eventually became an item.

Kay, I learned, had arrived in New York City from some God-fearing state hoping to find fame and fortune, but things hadn't quite gone according to plan. Plenty of men had 'auditioned' her in the bedroom but none had actually found her work. Out of luck and out of cash, Kay decided that rather than sleep with men in exchange for broken promises she would charge them up front. I wouldn't wish to incur the wrath and lawyers' fees of certain Hollywood actresses by naming names, so let's just say that Kay's plan was not original or a waste of time.

I had no thoughts of marriage or even a long-term relationship with Kay, so her 'profession' didn't bother me. In fact, I would often take her to find clients at hotels such as the Waldorf-Astoria, where normally she would have been refused entry. I would simply stroll up to the doors with Kay on my arm, say good evening to the door staff and walk in. Because I spoke with an English accent, the staff assumed that we were tourists and wouldn't bother checking if we were guests or had business at the hotel. Had Kay attempted to enter alone, she would most certainly have been turned away unless she could prove she was either a guest or had an appointment. Kay would sit alone in the hotel bar and within a very short time her looks would attract a wealthy businessman. More often than not, Kay would rejoin me an hour or so later and several hundred dollars wealthier. Occasionally, it would be a day or two before I saw her again, during which time she would have earned one or two thousand dollars.

Kay enjoyed the company of women as well as men. One night while we were out in Greenwich Village, she met a bisexual woman and soon after they began living together. I never did see Kay again.

The nearest gym to my apartment was in Times Square, so I would go there each day. I used to spar with Wilfred Benítez, who at seventeen years and five months of age became the youngest world champion in boxing history. Wilfred had won the welterweight title in 1979, but he had lost it to Sugar Ray Leonard by the time I met him a year later. During the period that I sparred with him, he did win the light middleweight title by defeating Londoner Maurice Hope.

Wilfred was managed by Jim Jacobs, who used to pay me $15 per round to spar with his fighters. It was often gruelling and painful but always very educational. I was also hired for three weeks to spar with Marvin Hagler while he prepared for his world middleweight title fight against Vito Antuofermo in Boston, Massachusetts. It was a wonderful experience for a young boxer like me. I sparred with Hagler for approximately 40 rounds during my time at the camp. Hagler actually mistook me for Antuofermo when I first arrived. It goes without saying that Antuofermo was a good-looking fella in his youth! The similarities between us did not end there; neither of us could get near Hagler in the ring. Antuofermo was knocked down in the third round of the title fight and his corner threw the towel in.

One morning in July 1981, I went to Gleason's Gym. I had $60 in my pocket and the rent was due on my room. I was rather hoping that I could arrange a prizefight or some sparring, otherwise I was going to end up homeless. As I walked towards the changing-rooms, Bobby Gleason beckoned me towards him.

'Are you still looking for a fight, kid?'

'Yes, I'm always looking for a fight,' I replied.

Gleason asked me to strip off and get on the scales. When I did so, he said, '168lbs. Can you make 160lbs?'

'No problem,' I replied.

I was then told to go and collect my passport, my boxing licence and enough personal effects to last me a week. I ran across town, packed my bag and had returned to the gym within an hour. Gleason gave me $100 in advance and a return aeroplane ticket. 'You're going to Caracas, Venezuela,' he said. 'It's in South America and you're fighting there next week.' He then led me out into the street and put me in a taxi. After handing the driver a $20 note, Gleason ordered him to take me to LaGuardia airport.

Later that day, I found myself sitting on an aeroplane next to an Englishman who worked at the British Embassy in Caracas. During the flight, we began talking and I told him

Wayne's parents,
Eric and Mary.

Wayne and his sisters,
Tracy and Lorraine.

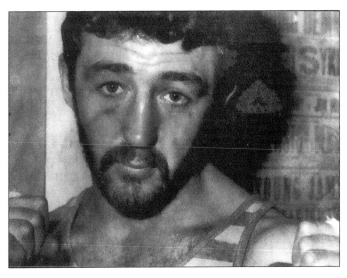

Wayne in the 1980s.

Wayne and former world middleweight champion
Alan Minter.

Wayne in reflective mood.

Wayne and Eugenio Monteiro, whom he discovered in
Cape Verde.

Lorraine, Tracy and Wayne in the '90s.

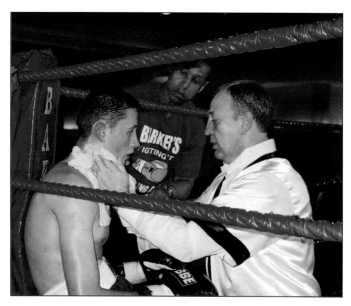

Wayne attending to Prince Arron between rounds.

Wayne and heavyweight champion Sir Henry
Cooper OBE (adjusting bow tie) at the
Midland Hotel, Manchester.

Wayne feeling the strain
while training.

Glamour model Nell
McAndrew and Wayne.

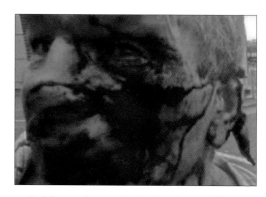

Celebrity Gypsy Paddy Doherty following
his fight with Johnny Joyce.

Wayne and friends from Yorkshire.

Wayne at the
Starlight Club
in Manchester.

Wayne and Claire at
the races (courtesy of
Claire Garnett).

Wayne being filmed for the *Faces* TV series next to the
ladder from which he fell.

that I was a professional boxer and was on my way to South America for a fight. 'Really? So who are you fighting?' the man enquired. Things had happened so fast that morning that it was one question I had failed to ask Bobby Gleason – but I was soon to find out.

ROUND SEVEN

Judas Kiss

AS THE PLANE taxied towards the airport building in Caracas, my fellow passengers began talking excitedly. At first, I thought everyone was pleased to have touched down safely, but it hadn't been what I would call a turbulent flight. I began looking around to see what was causing such a furore. In front of the airport building there was a line of soldiers all standing to attention. Behind them were banks of television cameras and a large group of what I assumed were reporters and photographers. In front of the soldiers, a long red carpet had been laid out in front of a terminal gate and our plane was taxiing towards it.

'There must be a pop star on board,' I said to the man from the British Embassy.

'Certainly some sort of dignitary. They don't do this for just anybody,' he replied.

As one of the air hostesses walked towards us, the man next to me began speaking in Spanish. He then looked at me and began to laugh.

'What's so funny?' I asked.

'Well, Mr Barker, the reception committee appears to be for you, because your opponent is none other than the Venezuelan national hero Fulgencio Obelmejias,' the man replied.

131

I initially thought he was joking, but I could tell from the beaming smile of the air hostess that I really was going to fight Fully Obel, as he was better known, a man who had fought Marvin Hagler for the world middleweight title just seven months ago. Fully Obel was indeed a national hero in Venezuela; he had represented his country at the Montreal Olympics in 1976 and his record prior to the defeat by Hagler was 30 fights, no defeats and 28 knockouts.

As I walked down the steps of the plane, a brass band began to play and members of the press began calling out, 'Señor Barker, Señor Barker!' Four officials greeted me and shook my hand as I reached the bottom of the steps, and then I was led down the red carpet to a waiting car. It suddenly dawned on me why Gleason had not mentioned my opponent. A week to get ready for a fight of this magnitude was ridiculous. But I was going to do what I had always done: think positive and believe that I would win.

I was taken by car directly to a press conference, where I was asked to pose for numerous photographs and answer questions about the forthcoming fight. I was then driven to the Hotel Hilton Anauco, which is in the heart of the financial district in Caracas. After being given a little privacy while I showered and changed, I was taken to see a man who resembled an obese Buddha. He was lying on a king-sized bed beneath a fan in the lounge of a fabulous penthouse. I have no idea who the guy was, but I was in no doubt that he was an extremely serious player in the city. He was surrounded by armed guards, none of whom dared to make eye contact with him.

The man looked about 50 years of age and spoke in short, sharp sentences. He said something in Spanish to the man who had driven me from the hotel and he then asked me in English for my passport. I took my passport out of my breast pocket and, before I could ask why he wanted to look at it, one of the guards snatched it from me. He then gave the passport to the Buddha and he put it in a drawer.

My driver was kind enough to translate what the man on the bed said. I learned that he was the promoter of the fight. I was to be paid $25,000 for the bout. I would only have Venezuelan people in my corner and anything they instructed me to do I was to adhere to. My passport was being kept until the fight was over. If I did not comply with any of the instructions I had received, I would not be leaving the country. When the driver had finished translating for me, everybody began to smile and I was given an ice-cold Cuba Libre – locally brewed rum and Coke. After I'd finished my drink, I was ushered out of the penthouse and driven back to my hotel.

Later that evening, I met an American named Mitt Barnes. He used to manage Leon Spinks, who had defeated Muhammad Ali to win the world heavyweight title. Mitt wished me good luck in the fight against Fully Obel and gave me his card, as he was flying back to the United States that night. 'If you're ever looking for a fight in the future, Wayne, ring me,' he said.

It's hard to describe the atmosphere in the national stadium that night in Venezuela. I was told that 15,000 fans were in attendance, but the noise they made as Fully Obel entered the ring sounded more like 50,000. I was doing my best to blank out the noise and concentrate on my opponent, but it proved difficult. When the bell rang for the first round, the crowd roared and Fully Obel moved across the ring to meet me. For every punch he threw, I hit him twice. I gave a good account of myself in that round; in fact, I think my performance was so polished it unnerved the promoter, as I noticed him glaring at me from his ringside seat.

After the first bell, my Venezuelan cornerman said, 'Look, you have got to take the fight to your opponent. Don't sit back and pick him off or you'll lose,' and like a fool I did as I was told. Fully Obel knocked me down three times in the second round. He didn't hurt me and he certainly didn't knock me out; he just caught me as I advanced each time. On each occasion, I was back on my feet after a few seconds. Unfortunately, the referee stopped the fight before the round had ended and moments later I was walking back to my dressing-room through the crowd. Disappointed? Perhaps, but the $25,000 I had been paid helped make the experience bittersweet.

When I arrived back at my hotel, people were shaking my hand and asking me to pose for photographs with them. It was rather surreal, so I decided to go to my room until things had calmed down. As I made my way down the corridor, a tall, beautiful girl was approaching me. I said hello to her and after a bit of outrageous flirting on my behalf she agreed to have a drink with me. The girl was American and was alone on business in Caracas. We went out that night and I ended up sampling cocaine. I don't condone drug-taking, but I was still young and impressionable. In South America, they don't mix cocaine with baking soda, amphetamines or any of the other shit that Europeans mix it with. They don't snort it up their noses either. In Caracas, there were little shops that you could go into where they served the drug in very small earthenware espresso-type cups. Large green coca leaves were cut up into small squares and used like tea in a small pot. When the potion had brewed, the liquid looked murky brown. This was then poured into one of the small cups and swallowed in two or three gulps by the customer. I consider it my moral duty to report that most of the customers I saw looked three times their actual age and their mouths, littered with black and broken teeth, resembled burnt-out villages. After drinking just one cup of this strange brew, I was totally wrecked. Not in a way that made me feel ill, though; in fact, I felt bloody marvellous. I spent the remainder of the night and most of the following morning showing my American friend just how good I did feel. When I awoke after a brief respite, she was still sleeping, so I grabbed my bag and made my way to the airport.

When I arrived back in New York, my landlord claimed that he hadn't thought I was returning and so he had re-let my room. My possessions were gone and no explanation was offered regarding their whereabouts. I wasn't too concerned, as I now had $25,000 and could easily afford a room and any deposit that might be required. I made my way to the Times Square Gym and gave one of the trainers a few hundred dollars. He had been kind enough to help me arrange fights when I had been financially embarrassed, and I wanted to repay him. After leaving Times Square, I booked into the Lexington Hotel, an exclusive establishment in Midtown Manhattan.

Now I had money I could think beyond looking for an immediate fight to pay my rent. I spent the evening considering my options. I had enjoyed my stay in New York City, but perhaps it was time to move on. The following morning, I rang Mitt Barnes and asked him if his offer still stood. He confirmed that it did and so that afternoon I boarded a plane to meet him in Kansas City.

Mitt picked me up from the airport and drove me to his home. It was a monument to the grim reality of the boxing game. Fighters win some and lose some, but their managers never fail to pick up a hefty wage for their troubles. The sprawling property, which was surrounded by 20 acres of woodland, overlooked a lake and had a gym in the basement that was superior to any that I had trained in.

In conversation with Mitt, I learned that he had not always been involved in professional boxing. He had been a truck driver and had opened Mitt's Amateur Boxing Club in the infamous Pruitt-Igoe housing project in St Louis, Missouri. Built in the 1950s, the housing estate had become internationally known for poverty and crime.

Barnes's gym attracted a 15-year-old boy named Leon Spinks. Spinks, who lived on the estate and had just left his broken home, showed real promise and so Barnes used to drive him to fights, pay his hotel bills and occasionally give him spending money. In 1976, Leon Spinks won a gold medal at the Montreal Olympics. Eight professional fights later, he had defeated Muhammad Ali and was crowned the heavyweight champion of the world.

Mitt explained that that was when all of Leon Spinks' troubles began. He earned $216,000 for the Ali fight and was told the rematch could be worth £4 million to him. Overnight, Spinks became a celebrity, and when requests for interviews and personal appearances poured in he went into culture shock. Spinks, the boy who had grown up in poverty, suddenly had the world at his feet. He spent $45,000 on a limousine fitted with a television and bar. A Cadillac Seville cost him $18,000, a Coupe de Ville $15,000; he spent $20,000 on jewellery, $75,000 on a house in Detroit and blew what was left on partying. He was arrested for possession of cocaine and cannabis, but he claimed that he had been framed and the charges were dropped. He had soon spent every cent of his $216,000 winnings and $250,000 he had received in advance for training expenses in the run-up to the rematch with Ali. Spinks was not the only one finding fame difficult. Barnes split acrimoniously with his protégé after being squeezed out as his manager.

Mitt told me that Spinks was never the same boxer after defeating Ali, and certainly his results were mixed after that. He struggled after leaving the fight game, too. At one stage he was living in a homeless shelter and in 2006 it was reported that he was working in McDonalds emptying bins. Spinks' story of rags to riches to rags is not unique in boxing; in fact, it is quite a common tale.

I stashed the money I had earned in Caracas away and began training hard in Mitt's gym. He provided me with free accommodation and the use of a modest car. It wasn't long before I was back to the peak of physical fitness. I felt and looked good. There was a gym at a nearby complex called the Four Seasons where I would often train. One day I was working on a punchbag when I noticed a woman who was sunbathing by the side of a swimming pool watching me. She was tall and leggy; she had blonde hair and was wearing a skimpy green bikini. After making eye contact several times, the woman walked over to me and introduced herself. She told me that her name was Carol Myers and after chatting for a while she agreed to meet me for a drink two days later.

If only I knew then what I know now, I would never have even spoken to her, never mind met up with her. Carol Myers, a woman nine years my senior, turned out to be more like Michael Myers, the psychotic character from the Halloween series of horror films. Unfortunately, I had no inkling and I fell for her charms hook, line and sinker.

Six weeks after meeting Carol, I married her at a registry office in Kansas City. It wasn't blind love. I had my motives and I found out later that Carol had hers. I wanted a green card, which would permit me to reside permanently in the United States, and marriage to an American citizen would ensure that I was eligible to receive one. Carol believed I was wealthy or was destined to become so and wanted every dollar she could possibly squeeze out of me.

Unbeknown to me, my father had been trying to trace me at this time. He had placed several adverts appealing for information about my whereabouts in boxing magazines and newspapers throughout America. Around the same time, legendary matchmaker Teddy Brenner, who worked for the

Top Rank boxing promotions company, contacted Mitt Barnes. Brenner said he had heard about me and asked if I would fight Teddy Mann from New Jersey. Mitt told Brenner that I was prepared to fight anybody, and so the bout was arranged to take place over ten rounds at the Sands Casino Hotel in Atlantic City, New Jersey. The same week that the fight was arranged, Mitt Barnes read one of my father's adverts in a boxing magazine and contacted him without telling me. He told my father that on Thursday, 5 November, I was taking on Teddy Mann and the fight was going to be shown live on television. 'Why don't you come over as my guest? Seeing you will give Wayne a big lift,' Mitt suggested. My father accepted the offer and a few days later he landed in America.

I was sitting in the lounge of my home eating my evening meal when I heard a tap on the window. When I looked around, my father was grinning manically and beckoning me to open the door. Shocked is perhaps understating how I felt at that moment, but when I realised it really was my father I was extremely happy that he had found me. I thought his search for me and arrival in America might have been the result of a family member falling ill, but my father was quick to assure me that everybody was fine.

However, it wasn't all good news; there was one issue that needed resolving. 'I know you have this fight lined up, but I need you to return to Manchester with me for a few days and then you can come back,' my father said. I asked why he wanted me to return and he explained that he had been contacted by the police about my non-appearance at court for the attempted murder charge. He had managed to fob the officer off by saying that I was fighting in America and had not been made aware of the date. 'They've adjourned the case, son. If you return, you can get it out of the way and get on with your life,' my father advised.

I have to admit that I felt extremely guilty. I had lied to my father about my innocence and, because I had previously been honest, he had believed me without question. Accepting all I had said, my father had then paid £12,000 to the court in order to secure my release on bail. I knew that if I failed to attend court my father would lose his money, which was a small fortune in those days. 'Stay here for a while and then go back to England,' I suggested. 'I will fetch you back over for the fight and we can discuss the problem then.' My father knew I was stubborn and that there was little point in arguing with me. He said, 'Fine, but you need to sort things.'

It felt good having my father around, but he returned to England after just four days. Shortly after my father's departure, Mitt Barnes set up a training camp for me in Newark, New Jersey, where I was to prepare for my fight with Teddy Mann. Funnily enough, our accommodation was in a nearby town called Wayne. My sparring partner in the training camp was a man named Bobby Czyz. He went on to win the light heavyweight title and the world cruiserweight title. Early in his career, Czyz had fought and defeated Teddy Mann, so Mitt thought he was the ideal boxer for me to spar with.

Five days before the fight, my father arrived at JFK airport in New York. I had warned him to be careful when he had cleared immigration, because back then New York was not a safe place. 'There will be a driver waiting for you. Look out for him and he will bring you out to me,' I had said. My father got off the plane with a suitcase under each arm and his Salford mindset in active mode. Paranoid because of my warnings, my father was not taking any chances. To him, he was entering a war zone and everybody and everything that moved was now the enemy. When he cleared immigration and walked out of arrivals, he saw a man holding a placard with his name on it. Striding over to the man, my father began firing questions: 'Eh, mate, what's your game? How the fuck did you know I was on that plane?' The man didn't have an opportunity to answer all of the questions my father reeled off in rapid succession, so he simply blurted out, 'Your lad sent me. I have to take you to his hotel.' After convincing my father that he was perfectly legitimate, the driver led him to his car.

'Can I sit in the front? I love American cars,' my father said as the driver opened the rear door.

'No problem, sir,' the driver replied.

Before getting into the vehicle, the driver took off his jacket, revealing a shoulder holster and handgun strapped to his body. 'What the fuck are you doing with that?' my father demanded to know as the man adjusted his seat belt. It turned out that the driver was an off-duty policeman who drove taxis on the side to earn a few extra dollars. His fears now allayed, my father demanded to drive the taxi to New Jersey, but the off-duty cop was equally forceful in his refusal. When my father knocked on the door of my hotel room, he was still muttering about the Yanks having no sense of fucking humour.

It was good having my father around me again. He would come to my sparring sessions, shouting encouragement and issuing threats whenever he thought I was falling short of the mark. At the weigh-in the evening before the fight, I could see that I had made my father very proud. Wayne Barker, the disruptive kid from Salford, was on stage surrounded by TV cameras and boxing luminaries such as Tim Witherspoon.

On the night of the fight, both Teddy Mann and I were interviewed in the ring, as the fight was being broadcast live on the ESPN channel. It's almost customary for boxers to talk themselves up by boasting that they are going to knock their opponent out, but such behaviour has never appealed to me. I have given respect where it's due and remained tight-lipped when the ignorant have left their manners at home. I was asked how I thought the fight would go and I explained that if I had the power to look into the future then I wouldn't be boxing for a living. The journalist was clearly unimpressed with my non-committal answers. When he asked if I was going to knock Teddy Mann out, I replied, 'I'll tell you after the fight.'

After the interview, I climbed out of the ring and went in search of my dressing-room. There were to be five fights that evening, mine and Teddy's being the main event. At the end of a long corridor, ten makeshift dressing-room cubicles had been made, one for each boxer appearing that night. Outside the cubicles, next to an exit door, was a long wooden table where a woman was doing her sorry best to look busy by shuffling papers. It was her job to pay the winner of each bout. The winner of my fight would pick up $15,000; the loser would not get anything other than damaged pride. Shortly before I was due to enter the ring, my father came to see me. He told me that I had to win. 'This is more than a fight, son. This is your future. Now get out there and do it,' he said.

As soon as the fight got under way, I knew that I was going to be tested. I don't mean that Mann was a superior boxer or that he was unusually powerful, he just kept moving away every time I stepped towards him. When you have trained and psyched yourself up for a fight, it's really frustrating if your opponent simply wants to bob, weave and otherwise dance around you. When Mann did throw a jab at me, the thumb on his glove was being used to poke my eye. Within a short period of time, the glove had perforated both of my eyelids. As I began to sweat, my eyes began to sting and within minutes I was barely able to see my opponent. I could neither see nor hit Mann now, and I was growing increasingly frustrated. When the bell went to signal the end of round five, I approached the referee and asked him to look at my eyes. 'He is blinding me. Do something about it,' I said. The referee didn't acknowledge my complaint; he just indicated that I had to return to my corner.

As I sat down on my stool, my father's head appeared at my side. 'What the fuck are you doing, Wayne? You need to be doing this, you need to be doing that,' he shouted as he gesticulated with his fists. To be honest, I hadn't even started to listen to my father. I knew exactly what I was going to do next.

'Forget about all of that. This fight will end this round,' I said.

'What are you on about?' my father replied.

'You'll see,' I said as I stood up to face Mann again.

When the bell rang to signal the start of round six, I walked into the centre of the ring and head-butted Teddy Mann full in the face. He went down as though he had been shot and blood poured from a wound above his eye. 'He is fucking down now!' I shouted as I stood over my opponent.

I knew that I would be disqualified, so I didn't bother hanging around to hear any announcements. I simply slipped through the ropes and made my way to the dressing-rooms. I didn't get changed. Instead, I just picked all of my clothing up and walked over to the long wooden table where the woman was still busy shuffling papers. 'Wayne Barker. I've come to collect my winnings,' I said. Barely looking up to acknowledge me, never mind attempting to question me, the woman pushed a large brown envelope towards me and, pointing at a box on her form, said, 'Sign here.' I scribbled on the paper, grabbed what should have been my opponent's winnings and made a beeline for the lift and my room on the tenth floor, where sanctuary awaited me.

After showering, I began to get changed, but I was

disturbed by hammering on my door. It was Teddy Brenner, the promoter, and he didn't sound too happy.

'What's going on, Wayne?' he shouted.

'Nothing's going on. Can't a man get dressed in peace? I'll be out in a minute,' I replied.

I allowed my father into the room after I had dressed and he asked me what I thought I was doing. 'The man didn't want to fight. He kept backing away and when he did throw anything forward it was his thumb in my fucking eyes. Bollocks to that. He didn't want to box, so I done him with my fucking head,' I replied.

My father looked at me in astonishment but then began to laugh. 'You crazy bastard. They're saying you've taken his winnings as well,' he said.

'It wasn't a boxing match and he ended up on the floor, so why not?' I reasoned.

Before my father could answer, I grabbed him by the arm and led him to the door. 'Say nothing and keep walking,' I said, before stepping out into the corridor to be confronted by a sea of angry faces. As my father and I walked through the crowd, people were trying to ask me questions, but I just kept my gaze fixed firmly ahead of me. When we began walking down the stairs, the crowd followed, so I stopped, turned around and shouted, 'Fuck off all of you! If any of you carry on following me, I will burst your fucking lips.' I noticed Mitt Barnes and my trainer, Lou Duva, so I beckoned them forward. The four of us then walked down the stairs, out of the venue and into a waiting car.

Mitt didn't say too much. He just asked the driver to take us to Lou's house and then sat staring out of the window at the passing traffic. When we arrived, Mitt asked everybody to sit in the lounge, as he wanted us to watch the fight again on the ESPN replay channel. Throughout each round, I pointed out how Mann had seemingly not wished to fight and how my vision was being impaired by the constant jabbing with his thumbs. Eventually, Mitt and Lou agreed that it had been a messy contest, but they in no way condoned me head-butting my opponent. The fight was written off as a bad day at the office and it and the prize money were never mentioned again.

The following day, we all flew back to Missouri. When my father and I arrived at my home in Lake Ozark, I somehow managed to avoid him learning that Carol was my wife. I had told my father that I didn't want him getting into any deep or meaningful conversations with her as she did not know that I was wanted for seriously wounding my former cell-mate. This ensured that my father kept any conversations with Carol brief and if she did begin talking about my past he would quickly change the subject. My wife subsequently found my father's presence in our home rather uncomfortable, so when I said that I would like to return to the UK for a couple of weeks with him she almost bundled me out of the door.

My father had explained to me that if I returned to the UK and answered my bail the £12,000 he had lodged with the court would be safe. 'All you have to do is show your face and once the case has been adjourned you can return here,' he said. I had agreed to do as he asked.

A few days later, I was sitting in my father's home thinking about my forthcoming trial for attempted murder. If convicted, I would be going to prison for a very long time. I decided therefore to make the most of the time I had in Manchester.

One afternoon, I was sitting in a gym on Oldham Road surrounded by old friends who wanted to know all about my adventures in America. Suddenly, a voice boomed out across the room, 'Eh, kid! Kid, I have been reading all about you in the *Boxing News*. Where's my 25 per cent for the fights you had in America?' Suited and booted, with a large cigar hanging out the side of his mouth, my former manager Nat Basso had entered the gym.

'You hungry bastard,' I replied. 'How do you work out you're due 25 per cent of any money I earned in America? I sorted out those fights without you even being there.' I could tell Nat wasn't happy with my answer, but he didn't respond.

The following morning, I received a letter from the British Boxing Board of Control stating that I had to attend a meeting at the Piccadilly Hotel.

'How did they know I was even back in the country?' I asked my father.

'Because Nat Basso is the secretary for the Central Area Council of the Boxing Board of Control,' he replied.

Suddenly, the letter made sense; Nat had asked the Boxing Board of Control to intervene in our dispute about the money I had earned in America. There was no way I was going to pay Nat, but my boxing licence was important to me, so I decided to attend and argue my case rather than risk a lengthy suspension from the sport.

When I arrived at the Piccadilly Hotel the following day, I was informed that Herol 'Bomber' Graham would be my representative on the panel. Herol is generally acknowledged as one of the best British boxers of the post-war era. When proceedings got under way, it was alleged that I owed my manager 25 per cent of the money I had earned while fighting abroad. I argued that Nat Basso had not been in America or Venezuela, I had paid the people who were and as far as I was concerned that was the end of the matter.

'But you were under contract,' the board members argued.

'Fuck the contract. He isn't getting paid,' I replied.

After shuffling their papers and passing one another notes, the board informed me that I was banned from boxing for three months.

'Make it six, if you like, because I'm flying back to America in the morning,' I replied.

Herol Graham laughed out loud and began clapping his hands. 'Nice one, man,' he said as I got up and left the room.

That night, I sat in my father's front room listening to the incessant ticking of the clock on the mantelpiece. My father sat opposite me, his head buried in the evening newspaper.

'I can't do this,' I said.

'Can't do what?' my father replied.

'I need to tell you the truth. It was me who hurt the guy in my cell,' I said.

My father seemed confused. He reminded me that I had pleaded my innocence to him from the outset.

'Work it out. Two men locked in an eight foot by twelve foot cell and one gets cut up – who else could have done it?' I explained.

My father stood up and bellowed up the stairs to my mother, 'Mary, pack Wayne's bag. He's going back to America in the morning.'

Early the next day, I caught a train to London, and by lunchtime I was flying back to the States and leaving the possibility of a lengthy prison sentence behind me.

Wayne Barker, unsurprisingly, had not featured much in the thoughts of Mitt Barnes since the Teddy Mann fight. I had taken Mann's prize money and disappeared to England, so Barnes might have been forgiven for assuming that I would not return. He had therefore concentrated on organising bouts for other fighters in my absence. When I returned to Lake Ozark, Mitt explained this to me and said that he wouldn't be able to find me any more opponents. I needed to work, so I thanked Mitt for all that he had done for me and went in search of unlicensed opponents in St Louis.

I did fight on a couple of shows, but there wasn't enough

work to provide for my wife and me. I was given the number of a man at Orange County Gym in Florida who was looking for fighters to spar with a promising boxer named Anthony Salerno. When I rang this man, he assured me that, given my experience, I would not only get regular sparring work but fights could also be arranged for me if I so wished. I thanked him and said I would get back to him once I had spoken to my wife. I wasn't expecting Carol to move from one end of the country to the other without some sort of debate, but when I mentioned it she agreed at once. Her father was a former naval officer and, unbeknown to me, he lived in Florida. Carol had been contemplating moving nearer to him for some time. We hired a trailer, packed our possessions into it and set off on the 1,165-mile journey to our new home.

We initially rented a flat but eventually purchased a beautiful Georgian apartment in a private complex that boasted tennis courts, a clubhouse and several swimming pools. Carol's father assisted us with the deposit, but I was soon able to pay him back. As well as earning money from sparring, I had created a lucrative business selling designer clothing.

While in New York, I had noticed young boys pushing railings full of expensive clothing through the streets. Some of these boys would go to the Times Square Gym, which I used, and I asked them to explain what it was they did with the clothing. Apparently, traffic was so heavy in New York at that time that it was more economical to walk stock across the city than it was to transport it by conventional means. I had kept in touch with the boys employed in this trade and rang them from Florida to ask if they ever acquired garments to sell. Initially, they refused to get involved, but within a few weeks I was driving a vehicle laden with brand-new designer clothing from New York to Florida. When I returned home, I went from door to door in the upwardly mobile neighbourhoods selling the garments. Beaming at bored housewives, I would say that I had just finished exhibiting the exclusive clothing at a fashion show and had learned I had been given one or two extra pieces in error by my employer. I was therefore able to sell the clothing at knock-down prices. What woman could resist such good fortune visiting her front door? If I had employed two additional salesmen, I couldn't have met the demand. I was taking home approximately $600 a day.

Life was good for me at this time. I was married to a beautiful woman, we lived in a beautiful home, I was earning good money and my boxing career was once more about to take off. I had been offered a fight against Norberto Sabater, a Puerto Rican super middleweight. Sabater was a decent boxer who had fought for the American middleweight title against Frank Fletcher, although he lost on points. I was really looking forward to the fight and began training in earnest at Angelo Dundee's gym in Miami.

Two weeks before the fight was due to take place, I returned home. I picked up the mail and wandered over towards the swimming pool, where my wife was sunbathing. I had received a letter from my mother and was still reading it as I approached my wife. According to my mother, nothing of note had changed in Manchester. Many of my former friends were either on the run or in prison.

When my wife saw me, she asked what I was finding so funny. 'Nothing really,' I replied. 'It's a letter from my mother. She thinks I'm like Ronnie Biggs living over here.' My wife had never heard of Ronnie Biggs and asked me who he was. I explained that Biggs and others had carried out what became known as the Great Train Robbery and that he had spent his life in exile avoiding the police while his associates served long prison sentences.

My wife still looked bewildered and asked what a fugitive

could possibly have in common with me. Sitting down beside her, I said, 'I am going to be honest with you. I am wanted in the UK for attempted murder.' To say Carol looked shocked would be a huge understatement; she slumped forward and gazed at me in vacant astonishment. I told her about the attack on Whittington but spared her the more grisly details. The fact that my victim had murdered a child appeared to excuse my actions to my wife. Although she was unhappy that I had failed to reveal my past, Carol agreed that I had been justified and we should therefore put the matter behind us.

Five days later, Carol and I went out for the evening. We had a few drinks, dined at a local restaurant and returned home at approximately 9.30 p.m. We made love and lay in bed afterwards listening to music. Eventually, we fell asleep. Just after midnight, I was awakened by the sound of somebody moving around outside my front door. I jumped out of bed and, despite being naked, strode down the corridor preparing to confront my noisy visitor. As I reached the front door, there was a huge bang and it and the door frame fell in on top of me. Lying beneath the door and its frame, I was struggling to sit upright.

'Put your hands on your head. Do not fucking move,' the men yelled as they levelled various handguns and a rifle at my head.

'How the fuck can I put my hands on my head without moving?' I asked.

It's embarrassing but true: I actually urinated because I was so afraid that these men might actually shoot me in the head. For all I knew, they had come to punish me or to reclaim the prize money I had stolen after the Teddy Mann fight. They were screaming obscenities and threats while remaining totally oblivious to any response I gave.

Eventually, when I was lying motionless, one leaned over me and said, 'Are you Wayne Barker?'

'I am.'

'You are under arrest.'

Relief swept over me. It was obviously the police. I looked up and saw my wife standing by the bedroom door. Her face told me everything I needed to know. She had betrayed me.

'Can I get dressed and cleaned up?' I asked the police officers.

'Sure, but don't make our job difficult. We will be watching your every move,' one of them replied.

As I passed my wife on the way into our bedroom, I asked, 'Why did you do this to me?'

'The money, honey. It's all about the money,' she replied, before turning her back on me.

A few minutes later, I was being led to a police car. As the engine roared into life, I could see my wife looking out from the bedroom window. It was to be the last time I would ever see her.

ROUND EIGHT

Homeward Bound

BETRAYING ME FOR the $7,500 we had in our joint account, our mortgaged home – which was essentially a debt – a decent car that was paid for and the rest of our possessions was hardly going to catapult my wife into the global rich list. Had I been a multimillionaire, the deceit and her Judas-like behaviour might have been a tad more palatable, if not just understandable, but I guess life is all about cruel lessons and learning from them.

I was taken to a central detention centre called Orlando Annex, where I was stripped, ordered to shower then doused in white powder, which I was informed was being used to delouse me. I rather hoped that this was purely a routine exercise, because as far as I was aware I had never had lice or any other insects residing in or on my person. Covered from head to toe in the white powder, I was directed to a counter where an inmate handed me underwear, a bright-orange boiler suit and a pair of flip-flops.

After putting on this prison garb, I was led to a large cage containing approximately 40 men who were all awaiting extradition to their native countries. Half of the cage was used as a dining area; the other was used for sleeping. I chose to live in the dining room rather than try to find a bed. The sleeping area stank of body odour and I noticed that some inmates were sharing the same bed. The dining room turned out to be reasonably comfortable. It boasted an eight-inch by twelve-inch view of the prison wall, a sofa and a television, which was never turned off.

Just as I was beginning to settle in to my new abode I was unexpectedly moved to Tampa Bay Annex, which was an almost identical institute to the one in Orlando. Three days after arriving in Tampa, I had a chain attached to my waist, hands and feet before being put on a bus that transported me and several other inmates to a deportation centre near Snapper Creek in Dade County.

As I entered the centre, I could see a huge chain-link fence that spanned the exercise yard. On one side were males, on the other females. After enduring the mind-numbing experience of being processed into the prison – which involved answering endless mundane questions about the time I had spent in America – I was taken to a dormitory and invited to choose a bed. Looking around at my fellow inmates, I didn't really fancy remaining in the room, never mind choosing a bed. I was the only white man present and some of the welcoming smiles I received indicated that not all of the thoughts my hosts were experiencing were pure. I am not suggesting that my cell-mates were homosexual, although many probably were. I believed that it was my white skin that was generating the hostile vibes that I was picking up on. I decided therefore to keep the possibility of confrontation to a minimum by keeping myself to myself.

Rather than sit in a room heavy with negative atmosphere, I decided to venture out into the main courtyard. Groups of inmates were huddled together deep in conversation and others strolled in circles around the yard, enjoying the Florida sunshine. I noticed a full-size baseball pitch adjacent to where I was housed. Fit and bursting with energy after being cooped up for days, I stripped off my shirt and began to run around the perimeter fence. After completing 40 laps, I stopped to catch my breath next to what was little more than a large wooden shed. Looking in, I could see inmates weightlifting, working out on punchbags and sparring in a dilapidated boxing ring.

Walking into the shed, I saw that a huge Cuban guy was standing in the centre of the ring swinging his fists wildly at an opponent. A crushing blow sent the man to the floor and the Cuban stood over him shouting abuse and obscenities. As soon as the man had been removed from the ring, another entered and he too was soon dispatched amid a flurry of flying fists. I thought the Cuban might have been a reasonable street fighter, but he didn't have a clue how to box.

Rather than just stand idly watching this bully beating up inmates, I worked out on a punchbag but kept one eye fixed firmly on him. When I had seen all that I needed to see – which didn't take long – I approached the ring and offered to fight him. Smiles from his entourage greeted me as I climbed into the ring. Banging his gloved fists together like some sort of brain-damaged Neanderthal, my opponent seemed convinced that I was just another lump of meat that he could punch around the ring at his leisure. As I advanced towards him, he began swinging his club-like fists towards my head. Bobbing and weaving, I was able to get in close and deliver devastating head and body shots without him being able to punch me once.

Looking at the spectators' faces, I soon realised that if I hurt the Cuban, I wasn't going to be leaving the ring alive. I continued to avoid his windmill-like punches, but I refrained from hitting him with any real force. After two rounds, the Cuban threw off his gloves and left the ring. He hadn't received the beating he deserved, but he had certainly been humiliated.

As I walked out of the shed, an old man said to me, 'Watch your back. You may have a problem.' When I asked the man what he meant, he explained that the Cuban controlled the deportation centre. 'He won't be happy that you've belittled him,' he said. 'Lots of people are in his debt for contraband and most would happily hurt you in exchange for having their debt rubbed.' I thanked the man for his warning and walked away.

Brave I may have been; stupid I will never be. I knew I could be stabbed in the back by a stranger, in my bed or in the showers, before I would have a chance to react. I wasn't going to risk serious injury, so I walked over to the nearest guard and said that I wanted to be put in solitary confinement or there would be trouble. 'If you don't agree to my request and there is trouble, I will not be held responsible for my actions,' I added. The guard eyed me with caution before ordering me to follow him. Less than five minutes later, I had been locked in a cell that boasted a single bed, a chair, a table and a television. It was barely comfortable, but it ensured my safety, and for that I was grateful.

The following week, I appeared in court, where bail was set at $100,000. I was an Englishman in America whom nobody really knew, so the possibility of a third party handing over so much money for my benefit was at best remote. I faced a grim choice: spend up to a year in solitary confinement and then get deported, or return to the UK immediately of my own free will. It didn't take me long to make up my mind. I telephoned my mother and asked her to book me a one-way ticket home from Miami. When I received confirmation that this had been done, I informed the prison authorities and said I was willing to leave America voluntarily.

A few days later, I was being escorted through Miami airport dressed in an orange boiler suit and shackled to two guards. A third guard walked in front of me and another one behind. People stopped and stared as I shuffled and rattled my way through the departure area. The guards boarded the aeroplane with me and refused to take off my chains until the doors were about to be closed prior to take-off. An air hostess eventually signalled to the guards and I was released from my shackles. 'Bon voyage, buddy,' one of my escorts said as they turned to leave the aircraft. I didn't reply. I just lay back in my seat, took a deep breath and closed my eyes as I exhaled.

I could feel my fellow passengers staring at me, so I pretended to be asleep in the hope I could avoid their inevitable questions. Pretence soon became a reality and we were five hours into the flight before I awoke. Interest in me from the other passengers had waned, and only one woman seemed to notice that I had woken up. 'Are you OK?' she asked. I told her that I was fine and, in order to save her asking further probing questions, I explained how I had ended up wearing the bright-orange jumpsuit. For the remainder of the flight, people bought me drinks and shook my hand for attacking Louston Pantry's killer. 'He deserved it,' they agreed unanimously. I just hoped that the judge who would eventually preside over my case would share their sentiments.

When the plane bounced down the runway at Heathrow airport, I immediately began to look for my reception committee. I knew the American authorities had been in contact with the British police and therefore I assumed that they would be waiting for me. I just didn't know if they would surround the plane or simply arrest me in the arrivals hall. I was allowed to leave the aeroplane without any intervention, so I collected my solitary bag from the luggage carousel and made my way to passport control.

The Department of Corrections in America knew what they were doing when they decided to make prisoners wear distinctive bright-orange clothing. Even Stevie Wonder could have spotted somebody wearing one of their boiler suits in the largest of crowds. As I waited to clear passport control, I noticed two detectives eyeing the queue. My sixth sense screamed that they had come for me, but they appeared to be oblivious to my telltale attire. As I flashed my passport and walked away from the immigration officers' booth, I heard a voice begin shouting, 'That's him! That's him in the boiler suit!' There was no point in making a dash for freedom, as my clothing made me the most conspicuous person in the south of England, never mind the airport. As I glanced over my shoulder, I saw a man gripping the arm of one of the detectives while pointing towards me and shouting. I couldn't help but smile. I had been so close to avoiding detection without even trying, but there's always one fucking jobsworth. I dropped my bag and waited for the detectives to approach me, read their arrest warrant and then take me to the cells.

That afternoon I was transferred to Bow Street police station in the West End of London before being put on a train back to Manchester with two officers as my escort. When we arrived at Manchester Piccadilly station, my father was there to greet me. He asked me if I was OK and if I needed anything, before warning my escorts to 'take care of my lad'. The following morning, I appeared at the magistrates' court, where I was remanded in custody to await trial for the attempted murder of Stephen Whittington.

From Florida to fucking Strangeways prison in less than a week – depressed doesn't begin to describe how I felt. As in every situation that I have faced in life, I tried to put the negative aside and look for positives. I concluded that, whatever the outcome of the court proceedings, the Whittington episode would finally be behind me and I could get on with my life. I was home, near my family, and, of course, I was back amongst my own kind. Unlike in Florida,

I knew exactly who could and couldn't be trusted.

HMP Strangeways at that time housed several of my old acquaintances, such as Lar Davies, Ian Massey, Chic Taylor and a one-time member of Manchester's infamous Quality Street Gang (QSG). In the '60s, '70s and '80s, the QSG were involved in armed robberies, long-firm frauds and protection rackets throughout the North-west. It has since been alleged that some members were heavily involved with the IRA.

For reasons known only to the prison authorities, large numbers of inmates were forced to have visits in a closed environment. The general population of most prisons enjoy visits sitting at a table opposite their family, friends and loved ones in a large hall or room. In Strangeways, I and others were put into cubicles where a glass partition prevented us from having any physical contact with our visitors and all conversations were monitored by prison officers. I felt that this was an unnecessary intrusion, not only for prisoners but for their visitors, too, so I asked the other inmates if they would join me in staging a peaceful protest.

They agreed, and so the next time we were allowed out into the exercise yard we sat down and refused to return to our cells. After three or four hours of inactivity from the prison staff, some inmates grew bored and trudged back into the prison wing, but myself and half a dozen others were determined to be heard, so we remained. At four o'clock in the morning, the bright security light that had been trained on us was switched off and the MUFTI (Minimum Use of Force Tactical Intervention) squad descended upon us. We were dragged off to our cells and locked up until the prison governor arrived later that morning.

One by one, we were taken to his office, where we were informed that we had breached several prison rules concerning good order and discipline. For these abhorrent acts, we were

157

going to be fined and shipped out to various prisons around the country. Ian Massey and I were taken to HMP Armley in Leeds, a place I hated from the moment I set eyes on it.

'I'm not having this,' I told the officer who began asking for my details in reception.

'Having what?' he replied.

'I'm not staying in this fucking jail, so you or whoever better move me,' I shouted, before picking up a chair and launching it at the main office.

Within an hour, I was on my way to HMP Durham, an establishment that was built in 1819 and which didn't appear to have changed much since. As soon as I walked into the reception area, I was reintroduced to the MUFTI squad, who threw me to the floor and clubbed me with batons. I was then dragged to solitary confinement and left in a heap on the cell floor. In the morning, I gazed forlornly around at my minimally equipped cell and wished I had at least given HMP Armley a chance.

I have to concede that I was a difficult man to deal with in those days. I couldn't be told what to do, and if a prison officer dared to even touch me I would threaten to snap his jaw. My rebellious streak resulted in me spending several months in solitary confinement. Eventually, the officers learned what they could and couldn't do without upsetting me, and a truce of sorts was reached. When the prison governor noticed that there hadn't been any incidents reported concerning me for some time, I was moved to the main part of the prison.

A man has to make a living, whatever situation he may find himself in and wherever that may be. Inmates are allowed to wear their jewellery in prison, and I noticed that many had designer watches and heavy gold chains. The average prison pay back then was £2.50 per week, so I knew that those who smoked and had other vices were struggling to make ends meet. I therefore offered to purchase their jewellery for a fraction of its worth. When I was given an item, I would pass it to my father during a visit, along with the owner's name and prison number. My father would then sell the item and send the inmate a postal order, which would be paid into his prison account. I was never going to get rich selling inmates' jewellery, but I was earning at least £2,000 per month, which was a reasonable wage back then.

As well as smuggling contraband out of the prison, my father would smuggle items in for me. All goods would be pre-ordered and ranged from bottles of spirits to legal and illegal smoking materials.

On one occasion, a Geordie ordered and received something from me but failed to pay. After a civil request to honour his debt from me was ignored, I went to his cell and battered him. Ten minutes later, I was being escorted back to solitary confinement, where I ended up confronting the prison officers who were attempting to lock me up. Stepping away from me, the officers pressed a panic-alarm button and advised me that it would be better for everybody if I just walked back into my cell and closed the door. I refused and warned the officers that if any of them took a step closer to me I would knock them out.

It started off as a distant rumbling of keys, chains and heavy boots clattering on a stone floor. As the sound intensified, I saw a wall of Perspex shields advancing towards me, behind which were irate-looking, baton-wielding officers. I ripped off my shirt and flung myself at the mass of flailing arms and boots that was descending upon me.

Some time later, I regained consciousness in what appeared to be a steel cage within a prison cell. I noticed that the prison governor was observing me.

'What the fuck have you put me in here for?' I asked.

'Behave like an animal in my prison, Barker, and you will

get treated like an animal,' he replied, without averting his gaze from my battered and bruised torso.

As I stood up, I asked the governor if I could just say one thing. 'Yes, Barker, you may,' he replied as he leaned towards the cage to hear me. When his head was within range, I lashed out with a left hook that connected beautifully with his chin and left him sprawled out on the floor.

Unfortunately, my elbow struck a bar of the cage when I punched the governor and the bone was chipped. The pain was intense, so when the prison officers rushed me in retaliation for assaulting the governor I was barely able to defend myself. I have no recollection of leaving HMP Durham. I just know that the following morning I awoke in the hospital wing at HMP Strangeways in Manchester. I was badly bruised and concussed, but I soon recovered and was reunited with my friends on the main prison wing.

In April 1983, I appeared at Manchester Crown Court for the attempted murder of Stephen Whittington. I denied the offence, but my legal team informed the prosecution that I was willing to plead guilty to a lesser charge of wounding with intent. My plea was accepted and I was sentenced to two years' imprisonment.

Shortly after being sentenced, I was transferred to HMP Preston, where I was given a job as a gym orderly. From eight in the morning until six in the evening, I was free to train seven days a week. I taught both prison officers and inmates to box and in return they would give me small gifts. The prison officers' wives would make me cakes and the inmates would give me fruit, chocolate or vodka.

Twelve months after being sentenced, I was granted parole and subsequently released. It was good to be out. I had no outstanding matters with the police, I was extremely fit and I was raring to get back into the ring. After visiting my parents, I made my way to the gym where my manager Nat

Basso and a few of my friends had gathered to welcome me home.

Among those friends was Frank Evans, the Salford bullfighter. Frank was born and bred in Salford. His father was a butcher. When he was a child, Frank was taken to a slaughterhouse, where he witnessed cows and bulls suffering terrible deaths. Frank's father, who was stationed in Gibraltar during the Second World War, often told his son about the bullfights he had watched when he had visited neighbouring Spain. As a result of his experiences, Frank grew up believing that the killing of a bull in the ring was somehow nobler than butchering it in a slaughterhouse; the bull was at least given the opportunity to fight back. Aged 19, Frank attended a wedding in Spain, where he watched his first bullfight. The experience captivated him, and he enlisted at a bullfighting school in Valencia. He went on to be ranked number 63 in the world out of 10,000 bullfighters. I like Frank. He is a real character, whose desire and bloody-minded attitude got him through many difficult situations in his life.

Nat Basso appeared pleased to see me. He asked if I was fit enough and willing to fight. When I told him that I couldn't wait to get back into the ring, he immediately began telephoning his counterparts in the hope of arranging a bout.

In February 1984, I fought a Glaswegian named John Hargin at the Holiday Inn in Liverpool. It had been nearly three years since my last professional fight, against Teddy Mann in Atlantic City, so I could have been excused for having a little ring rust, but I still managed to knock Hargin out in the fourth round.

A month later, I fought Paul Murray from Birmingham at the Kings Hall in Manchester. I am sure Paul won't mind me saying that he was a bit of a journeyman. He fought a total of 109 fights and lost 80. His superior experience in the ring soon tired me, though, and I wasn't as aggressive as I should have been. I spent much of the fight with my back on the ropes, picking out shots as he advanced towards me with his head down. I won the bout on points, but it wasn't my greatest performance in the ring.

Shortly after that fight, I had a bridge fitted, as my teeth had been damaged by all the fighting I had done over the years. I felt pretty rough for some time afterwards, so I didn't bother training. When I received a call offering me a fight against a guy from Wolverhampton named Deano Wallace, I should have declined. However, I was assured that it would be an easy pay day, as he had been knocked out during his last fight in the third round. The bout took place at a packed Kings Hall in Belle Vue, Manchester. I wish I had stayed at home in bed. I punched myself out within four rounds and in the sixth I got knocked down. As I got to my feet, I looked around at the crowd who were baying for my blood and thought, 'I'm getting paid £400 for this. Do I really need it?' When the referee signalled for Wallace and me to continue boxing, I walked to the edge of the ring, climbed through the ropes and strolled to my dressing-room.

I had embarrassed myself and swore that I would never enter a ring again. That night, I went out and got drunk. I was a ball of emotion, embarrassed and angry with myself for thinking I could just turn up and fight without training. As the great Muhammad Ali once said, 'The fight is won or lost far away from the witnesses, behind the lines, in the gym, and out there on the road, long before I dance under those lights.' In a rather pathetic attempt to prove to myself that I still had what it took, I got into two fights that night and knocked both men out. Standing over their motionless bodies didn't help; I still felt somehow inadequate.

The Gunfighter Syndrome that my grandfather had told me about began to haunt me. Wayne Barker the fit young man was rapidly turning into Wayne Barker the tired old man. My mind might have been resisting the change, but my body was clearly succumbing to time's every whim. To add insult to my aching bones, I was being paid a pittance for my endeavours.

I opened a scrapyard in Cheetham Hill. I would pay local car thieves £100 to steal a car at night and leave it smashed up near my yard. The following morning, I would ring the police to report the vehicle and they would pay me a £100 recovery fee. The insurance assessors would then inspect the vehicle and more often than not they would declare it to be a write-off. That meant it would cost more to repair the car than to replace it. I would then offer the insurance company a nominal fee to purchase the car for scrap. However, the vehicles would rarely be scrapped; I would strip them for parts, which I would then sell via *Auto Trader*. I was earning thousands of pounds from this scam. For example, within two months I was able to purchase a brand-new Rolls-Royce.

One afternoon, a young lad drove into my yard in a brand-new Granada 2.8i Ghia X. At the time, this was the motor vehicle to own, but I knew that it was way out of the price range of this particular individual. I asked him whose car it was and he said it was his. I did a quick check on the number plate and learned that it was registered to a Charles Mitchell in Aberdeen. Further checks revealed that Charles Mitchell was the proprietor of Mitchell's Self Drive, a national vehicle-hire company. I jumped in my car and drove to a Mitchell's depot near Strangeways prison and scribbled down half a dozen of their car registration numbers. I then returned to my yard where I ran an HPI check on the vehicles. Anybody can do these checks. You ring a registered agent and for a small fee they will tell you a car's complete history. Every vehicle came back as being registered to Charles Mitchell in Aberdeen, but more importantly every check showed that the vehicles had been paid for outright. That is extremely unusual, as most car-hire company fleets are stocked using lease or credit facilities.

I began hiring the vehicles and having identical vehicles stolen. Overnight, they would be placed side by side in a garage and their registration plates and any other identifying features would be switched. The following morning, the stolen car would be returned to Mitchell's cloned as their hire car. I would then have a set of number plates made for the hire car, tax it and an associate would put it in Brighouse auction in West Yorkshire. I would attend the auction later that day and outbid anybody who tried to buy the vehicle. As I was buying my own vehicle, I only stood to lose the commission fee the unwitting auctioneers would charge. In return for that small fee, I effectively owned a bona fide high-value 'straight' car, which I was free to sell on.

Detective Sergeant Hulse from the stolen vehicle squad in Longsight, Manchester, soon got to hear what I was up to and swooped on me. I was taken to a police station and led into an operations room, where I saw that the walls were adorned with hundreds of photographs of me. 'Is that you in the photographs, Mr Barker?' the officer asked. Theatrically squinting my eyes, I replied that the man did bear a striking resemblance to me, but I couldn't be absolutely sure. I asked the officer why he had taken so many photographs of the man that might or might not be me.

'Because you have bought all of these cars, Mr Barker,' the policeman replied as he pointed to a wall covered in more photographs.

'The only cars I buy are out of the auctions. I have all the receipts,' I said, trying to look confused.

'That may be the case, but they are all stolen. They are what we call ringers, Mr Barker,' the officer said.

Feigning innocence, I asked the officer what stolen cars had to do with me. Staring intently at me, he said that 98 vehicles had been hired from Mitchell's in the North-west region. All of these vehicles had been cloned with stolen cars and had ended up being sold at auctions. Saving the best for last, the officer stepped towards me and said, 'What is surprising, Mr Barker, is that you have successfully bid on every single one of them.'

I told the officer that his evidence sounded very circumstantial and nothing he had said proved that I had committed any offence.

'Can you explain why you have never bid on any vehicle other than stolen ones at the auction, Mr Barker?' the officer asked.

'If you're not going to charge me with any offence, then I think it's time to end this particular conversation,' I said, before walking out of the room and the police station.

Anybody foolish enough to venture into my yard was at risk of being ripped off. I would advertise in *Auto Trader* magazine parts for top-of-the-range vehicles, such as Ferraris, that I didn't have, and as soon as somebody took the bait they were snared. For instance, a guy from the Isle of Man rang me one day about a Ferrari gearbox that I had advertised. I told him there had been a lot of interest but if he paid me a deposit I would keep it for him. Later that day, £1,000 was paid into my bank account. When the man came to collect the gearbox, I told him that it had been sold by mistake and offered him a credit note instead of returning his cash. He went to the police to complain, but there was nothing they could do, as I hadn't broken any law. The credit note was worthless, unless, of course, the man wanted to haul a load of scrap parts back to the Isle of Man.

At the bottom of the road where my parents lived, there was a pub. The landlord's son had been involved in a road traffic accident and his sister Julie had called in my yard one afternoon asking if I had a replacement door in stock for his vehicle. I took £80 from her and said that I would call her as soon as I had sourced one. After a week, her polite phone calls requesting news of her brother's car door had turned into hate-filled rants threatening violence. I had become used to such phone calls from my customers, so, rather unwisely, I took little or no notice of her.

The Alsatian dog that guarded my yard can only be described as a rabid killer. Nobody could get near it without being mauled and bitten, except for me. I was therefore surprised to discover one morning that Julie had scaled the wall of my yard and avoided being savaged by the dog as she smashed windows in vehicles and my office. I didn't know that she was responsible for the damage at first, but she rang me to say that if she didn't get her door my yard would be getting more of the same. I laughed at her gall and assured her that the door would be ready to be picked up by closing time that day. There was, however, one condition.

'And what might that be?' Julie enquired.

'You only get your door if you agree to come out for a drink with me,' I said.

To my surprise, Julie agreed. Following a whirlwind romance, we set up home together in Eccles and shortly after that she fell pregnant.

I suppose my story could have ended there. A new partner, a new home and a baby on the way should surely have equalled everlasting bliss. But Wayne Barker's fire burned strong, and I wanted more, so I involved myself in every act of criminality that I thought might make me wealthy.

Using a false name, I opened a new scrapyard business in Levenshulme, called Star Breakers. I then rented four plots of land and filled them with stolen cars that I had recovered using the insurance scam.

There was a man whom I'll call David Riley who had a

scrapyard off Oldham Road in Manchester. I was informed by a friend that Riley was experiencing financial difficulties. His yard was supposedly full of stolen vehicles and parts, so one Saturday morning I paid him a visit in the hope that I could help. When I climbed out of my Range Rover with a huge muscular black guy in tow, I could see that Riley was worried. Those he owed money to had obviously been warning him that something could happen to him.

'Hi, my name's Wayne,' I said, extending my hand. 'I've heard you have a cash-flow problem and I would like to make a bid for your stock.'

'Well, I'm not really in trouble for a few quid, but I'm always willing to listen to offers for my stock,' Riley replied.

I walked around the yard scribbling notes and figures on a writing pad. I concluded that if I paid £50,000 for the stock I'd be stealing it. Without any facial expression, I looked at Riley and said, 'You've got one bid and one bid only. I'll give you £20,000 and I'll clear the place out as soon as is physically possible.'

Riley thought about it for a couple of minutes and then said, 'Right, you're on.'

Within the hour, I had two lorries at the yard and half a dozen men. I told them to remove all of the vehicles' engines first, then the alternators and any other expensive parts and leave the panels until last. By Sunday evening, only the shells of the vehicles remained.

Unbeknown to me, the police had for some time had Riley's yard under observation, as they suspected he dealt in stolen car parts. On the Friday night, before I arrived on the scene, the police had decided that they had enough evidence to arrest Riley. They stood down the surveillance team in preparation for a raid on the Monday morning. At the same time as the police were pulling up outside the yard, a lad whom I had sent to pay Riley arrived. Fortunately, when he saw the heavy police presence he drove away in the opposite direction and rang me.

Riley later told me that when the police poured through his gates they came to an abrupt halt when they reached his stock of vehicles. 'Where are all the engines and parts, Riley? We know they were here on Friday,' they said. Riley denied all knowledge of anything other than what was currently in his yard, and the police were forced to leave empty-handed.

Riley's joy was, however, short-lived. I explained to him that I had saved him from serving at least five years' imprisonment and therefore I felt I should be rewarded. I told him I wasn't going to pay him the £20,000 for the stock but I was prepared to give him a job selling it. Reluctantly, Riley agreed and, in doing so, made me a lot of money.

An old Traveller once told me that if somebody ever ripped me off I shouldn't fight them. I should bide my time, let them think I was an easy touch and then rip them off for twice as much. It was a lesson I understood and one I employed many times.

A car dealer whom I'll call Tanner once offered to sell me a three-carat diamond ring. Tanner was a friend of the infamous Manchester villain Jimmy Swords, whom I knew, so I didn't think he would try to rip me off. Regardless, I am no mug, so I asked Tanner if he would bring the ring around to my home. He agreed, but what he didn't know was that I had a diamond/moissanite tester at home. These are electronic devices that are able to tell the difference between fake and genuine diamonds. When Tanner arrived, I took the diamond from him and tested it. It was a fake.

'How much do you want for it?' I asked.

'Three thousand five hundred pounds,' Tanner replied.

I nodded my head and asked Tanner if he had anything else for sale. He offered me a motorhome, two static caravans, three valuable paintings, jewellery, five gold watches and the deeds to a lock-up garage. I knew Tanner was a car dealer and I explained that I had a yard full of salvaged vehicles. 'I have a 1983 Ford Capri 2.8 Injection Special, a 1984 Supersport Bravo and six other high-value vehicles that I will part-exchange with you,' I said. Tanner, still convinced that he was dealing with a mug, stuck his hand out and said, 'You have a deal.' I gave him all the documentation relating to the vehicles and typed out a bill of sale, which he signed. An hour later, a few lads who worked for me had been to Tanner's yard and picked up the items that I now owned.

The following morning, Tanner sent eight drivers to my yard to pick up the vehicles that he now owned.

'What are you doing here?' I asked.

'We've come to drive away Tanner's cars,' one of the men replied.

'You won't be driving them anywhere,' I said. 'What you will need are car transporters.'

The lads looked totally bewildered, so I explained that the cars did not have wheels or engines – they were simply shells.

Thirty minutes later, my phone rang; it was Jimmy Swords. 'You can fuck who you like, but you're not fucking my mate,' he said.

'Your mate's been fucked and he is staying fucked for trying to rip me off,' I replied. I told Jimmy that if he didn't like it I would gladly fight him. 'I can come to you or you can come to me,' I shouted. The phone went dead and I thought no more about it. As my mother used to say, if you cannot keep hold of something, you didn't deserve it in the first place.

I invested my ill-gotten gains in a car pitch called Chariots in the town of Haslingden, which is about 15 miles north of Manchester. I was soon selling stolen cars with false number plates, so it wasn't long before the police began investigating the business.

Rather than waiting for the police to arrest me, I packed

my bags and informed Julie that we were moving to Wales. To say that Julie was unhappy would be an understatement in the extreme. She was pregnant and wanted to be near her family rather than living a Bonnie-and-Clyde-type lifestyle. I could understand her point, but my argument was that I didn't want to be in prison when she gave birth, and eventually she agreed. We settled in a village on the outskirts of Caernarfon in North Wales. I knew a few of the Travellers in the area, and I started work with them immediately. I was laying tarmac, felling trees and collecting scrap – nothing too lucrative, but I found it enjoyable. In fact, I remember the months that Julie and I spent in Wales as happy and carefree.

Before leaving Manchester, Julie had begun attending antenatal classes at the Hope Hospital. Rather than alert the police to my whereabouts by registering in Caernarfon, Julie used to travel back to Manchester for her appointments. However, the police were tipped off that Julie was still with me and they followed her from the hospital back to Caernarfon. Fortunately, rather than returning directly to our home, Julie visited a friend and a day later the police swooped on the address only to find that I had never lived there.

Undeterred, they began making enquiries in and around the town, so I began preparing to move. Vernon Bassett's son Ned was aware that I had arranged to withdraw several thousand pounds from a building society one morning, as I was going to purchase a truck. Vernon had always treated me well when I worked on his fairground several years earlier, but I always got the impression that his son was jealous of our relationship. For whatever reason, Ned informed the police that I was going to be at the building society at 9.30 on one particular day. When I walked in just before the allotted time, I told the cashier who I was and what I had come for. The account was in the name of Wayne Lee, but the police would have guessed that that was just one of several pseudonyms I used. The cashier looked up when I said the name, hesitated and then mumbled an apology, saying my appointment had been changed to 10.30. I thanked her and walked out into the street.

I instinctively knew that something was wrong, so I began walking back to my vehicle. As I approached the car, I could see that the lad who had been driving me was talking to a man. I began walking faster, but when the man saw me he walked off down the street.

'What did he want?' I asked the lad as I reached my car.

'He's a policeman and he wanted to know if I knew anybody from Manchester,' he replied.

While we were talking, a man tapped me on the shoulder and said, 'Have you dropped this pound coin?' Without thinking, I put my hand out to take the money and the next thing I knew I was in handcuffs. I was subsequently sentenced to two years' imprisonment for fraud and vehicle theft. Julie, unsurprisingly, was far from happy.

During our first visit at HMP Strangeways, I had to endure listening to her quite rightly complaining that I would miss our baby's birth. Once I had conceded that that was wrong, I was then verbally frogmarched into admitting that children need stability and parents who are committed to each other. I could see the next subject rising like a storm cloud, but there was no way I could avoid it and, to be honest, at that time I didn't wish to. In fact, I welcomed the idea of marriage.

Julie contacted the prison and requested that I be granted day release so that we could be married. The ceremony was booked to take place at Jackson's Row registry office in Manchester. I had genuinely been looking forward to the day, but I began to have my doubts. By the time I opened the registry office door and entered, I just knew I couldn't go through with the wedding, not while I was in prison.

Julie wasn't the only thing on my mind that day. My father had told me that after I left Manchester to go on the run Jimmy Swords had turned up at my yard, which my father was looking after. My father had asked Jimmy what he wanted.

'I want to give your lad a slap,' Jimmy replied.

'Give my lad a slap?' my father said. 'Get a grip of yourself. He would batter you all over the road if he was here now. Now get the fuck out of here.'

Jimmy left the yard, but my father had warned me that I should expect trouble on my release.

ROUND NINE

Duck, Dive, Bob and Weave

LIKE ALL RED-BLOODED men, I would often revel in my female partners' mistakes, but I have never rejoiced at a mishap like I did on the day I was due to be married. When booking the ceremony, Julie had been asked if I had been married before and, forgetting my American wife, she had replied no. As I entered the registry office with my prison escort, I could see by Julie's stern expression that all was not well.

She hissed in my ear, 'Wayne, they're going to ask you if you've ever been married before. What are you going to say?' Waves of relief washed over me. I pulled the straightest face possible, stepped back and said, 'I can't lie or our marriage won't be legal.'

There was absolutely no question mark over my love for Julie. I can confidently say that I had never loved any woman like I loved Julie at that moment, and there had been a few. I just didn't relish the idea of getting married while serving a prison sentence. Julie begged me to sweet-talk the registrar, but I couldn't give her much hope. 'These people won't break the law for a prisoner,' I said.

The registrar called all interested parties into a large room. As he asked Julie and me for identification, our addresses and the answers to other mundane questions, I was trying to speed-read his form for a question about previous marriages. It didn't appear to be there, but the registrar looked up over his glasses and smiled as he said, 'No previous marriages? Is that correct?'

Trying my very best to sound disappointed, I replied, 'Not in this country, no.' The registrar put down his pen and asked if I had ever been married previously in any country.

'I was married in America. But that doesn't count over here, does it?' I replied.

'Very much so, Mr Barker. It matters very much indeed,' he said. 'In the circumstances, I suggest a short break while I seek advice.'

A short break turned into a nearly four-hour wait, during which time I was given free rein by my escorts to roam around the registry office and mingle with my guests. Eventually, the registrar announced that the marriage ceremony would have to be cancelled.

I cannot say who was more upset, Julie or my two prison escorts. 'You must have known, Barker. You've done this for a day out, haven't you?' they said. All the way back to Strangeways prison, the officers bitched and moaned at me for wasting their day.

A few days after my aborted wedding, I was moved from Strangeways to HMP Haverigg in Cumbria. Personally, I wouldn't call the establishment a prison. It was a disused RAF camp inhabited by shoplifters and an assortment of similarly petty crooks. As soon as I had left the reception area, I was warned not to venture down the paths between the accommodation huts. When I enquired why I should be in fear of walking anywhere, I was informed that the paths, known as 'mugger's alley', were the territory of two Liverpudlians who supposedly controlled the jail. Seconds later, I was strolling down mugger's alley in search of trouble.

When I was between two of the buildings, a stocky man

stepped out in front of me and attempted to wrap a long sock full of snooker balls around my head. I ducked and punched my attacker as hard as I could in the solar plexus. He gasped for air and fell to his knees as another man appeared and took a swing at me. A beautiful combination of punches sent him sprawling into a wall, where I smashed his ribs with a salvo of body shots before allowing him to join the other chump at my feet. As I stepped over the men who had once controlled the jail, a prison officer appeared and began shouting frantically into his radio for help. I raised my hands to indicate that help wasn't needed and walked towards him. Moments later, I was surrounded by half a dozen baton-wielding officers who then escorted me to the block.

The following morning, I was taken back to Strangeways and put in a single cell, as, they said, they did not want another Stephen Whittington on their hands. Approximately one week later, I was taken to the reception area and told that I was being moved to HMP Preston.

While I was waiting for the necessary forms to be completed, an inmate who worked on reception approached me.

'Have you got anything you want to say to me?' he asked.

I had never spoken to this guy in my life. 'Why would I have anything to say to you?' I replied.

He claimed that I had called him a grass and began talking in a threatening manner in front of the other inmates who were sitting around me. 'Why are we having this conversation? If you think I have called you a grass, do something about it. You are a fucking grass. There you go. I've said it now, so let's resolve the situation,' I said, jumping to my feet.

The man backed away from me as two prison officers entered the room and asked if there was a problem. Nobody replied and shortly afterwards I and the other inmates who'd been present were loaded onto a coach and taken to HMP Preston.

As soon as we had been processed at reception, we were allocated cells on the induction wing. All prisons have induction wings these days. Inmates are locked up for seven days and are only allowed out of their cells periodically to answer pointless questions during pointless form-filling exercises. 'Do you now or have you ever had any sexually transmitted diseases?' 'Are there any pets locked in your home?' 'What job if any did you do outside?' Most prisoners answer the latter with a brief description of their crime: 'Last job? Er, I burgled a shop in the High Street.' Who actually benefited from a week of meaningless interrogation was the most difficult question I actually had to consider.

At the end of my induction week, I packed my personal possessions and waited to be transferred to one of the main prison wings. I could hear cell doors being unlocked, prison officers barking orders and doors being slammed, so knew I didn't have much longer to wait. When I heard my neighbour's cell door being opened, I picked up my possessions and stood waiting for the officer to unlock my door. I could hear the jangling of keys, but the sound of a cell door being unlocked came from my other neighbour's door rather than mine. I banged on the door and shouted to the officer that he had forgotten to unlock me. Moments later, the hatch in my door opened and a voice said, 'I haven't forgotten you, Barker. You're staying here, son.' The hatch then slammed shut and I could hear the officer's boots clicking on the highly polished floor as he walked away.

I had no idea what game I was being forced to be a part of, but I wasn't going to complain. That above all was what they wanted me to do. I just had to sit down, smile and pretend their childish behaviour was not bothering me. The following morning, my cell door opened and a grinning prison officer informed me that I was being moved to HMP Walton in Liverpool. I hated Walton jail with a passion. The cell they put me in stank, as did the inmate I was supposed to share it with. 'Get yourself some soap,' I shouted as I threw the filthy urchin around the walls before dumping him unceremoniously outside the cell. Within the hour, I had been moved to another wing and placed in a single cell. I still hated Walton jail. The food was slop, so I lived on beans and bread. I rarely spoke to anybody, and when I did it was strictly because it was a necessity.

One morning, I was strolling around the exercise yard when I heard my name being called. I approached the prison officer who had been calling out for me and asked him what he wanted.

'Do you want the good news or the bad news, Barker?' he asked.

'I'll leave the decisions to you, as you're the man with the keys,' I replied.

'The bad news is you're leaving us and the good news is you've been granted parole.'

I took the paperwork confirming my release from him and returned to my cell. Everything suddenly made sense to me now. The day I had left Strangeways, my parole application had been approved and the form stamped. The day I had left HMP Preston, my parole had been approved and stamped. I might well be wrong, but I truly believe that the incident at Strangeways and the decision to keep me on the induction wing had both been engineered to make me react so that I would not get parole. The attack on Whittington all those years ago had obviously caused the prison department or its employees more trouble than I had imagined.

I was released from HMP Walton on 23 July 1986. I remember the date simply because it was the day that Prince Andrew married Sarah Ferguson. The life I had left behind when I entered the prison system bore little resemblance to the one that now greeted me. My son James was nearly a year old and I felt robbed because I had missed so many memorable milestones in his short life. I had wanted to name him Eric, after my father, as they shared the same birthday, but my father had said that it wasn't a good idea as he had been 'an unlucky bastard', so it had been decided in my absence that my son would be called James after my grandfather. I was gutted, to be honest, but by the time I came out of prison it was too late to do anything about it. I should not complain about my situation. I had committed the crimes and therefore I had to do the time, albeit reluctantly.

I wasn't thinking about the future as I made my way to the prison gate that morning. I was thinking about Jimmy Swords and how he had told my father that he was going to give me a slap. When I stepped outside the prison, I saw that my father was waiting for me in a car across the street. I got in and asked him to drive me to Jimmy Swords' car pitch, where we found a few of his friends hanging around. 'Where's Jimmy?' I asked. The men said that he had gone out and wouldn't be returning until much later. 'Tell him Wayne Barker is looking for him. I want him to give me the slap he has been telling people he's going to give me,' I said.

I didn't hear anything from Jimmy, but approximately six months later I bumped into him in the office of a mutual friend.

'I want a word with you,' Jimmy said.

'Good, because I want to punch you all around this yard. Get outside!' I shouted.

Jimmy began saying that I had been in the wrong for ripping off his friend Tanner, but I wasn't interested. 'You have had your day, old man. Get outside. I want you to give me the slap you've been telling everybody about,' I said.

Jimmy sat down and said, 'Just forget it. There's no speaking to you.'

As far as I was concerned, he had backed down from a fight and so that was the end of the matter. He wouldn't be threatening me again.

From painful personal experience, my father knew that I would find it tough getting back on to my feet again after a stint inside. He wanted to help, particularly as I now had a family of my own and was showing signs of settling down. He therefore purchased me a Bedford TK lorry, which I needed to continue running my scrap business. The other good news that he had for me was he had managed to keep my yard open and running while I had been incarcerated. I was pleased because the yard was a magnet for mugs and their money.

A guy came to the yard the day after I had been released and offered to sell his Mercedes SL for £60,000. I was at my parents' home at the time and one of the lads who worked for me rang and told me about the offer. Without really thinking, I told the lad to send the guy round to my parents' house. When he arrived, I looked around the vehicle and said that I would like to purchase it for Julie. After a little haggling, the guy agreed to sell it to me for £58,000. I called Julie to come out of the house, gave her the keys and told her to test-drive her new vehicle while the man and I sorted out the payment and paperwork. I invited the man into the house, he filled out all of the necessary paperwork concerning the sale and change of ownership, and I wrote out a cheque for £58,000. Before he had arrived, I had written on the back of the cheque, 'Please do not present this cheque at my bank unless authorised by me to do so.' The man checked the amount of money I had written on the front of the cheque, folded it and put it in his top pocket. We shook hands and he then left in a friend's vehicle.

The following morning, the man attempted to pay the cheque into his account, but the bank clerk queried the inscription that I had written on the back. When I received a call from the bank manager asking me what it meant, I said that it was a clause in the contract of sale. I added that the man had not sought my permission to present the cheque and he was therefore in breach of the contract and the cheque should not therefore be honoured. The man contacted the police, but they advised him that it was a civil matter and they could not get involved. I was taken to court, but as the man was in breach of contract I won the case and kept his car.

Shortly afterwards, I purchased 24 Arbroath Street, Droylsden, which was a fire-damaged property. With the help of a few friends, I transformed the terraced house into a luxury abode within a few months, after which Julie and I and our son James moved in.

I don't know if I was undergoing a midlife crisis or if the hunger I had had for boxing had never really subsided, but for some reason I felt a real urge to fight once more. I began training hard and had soon returned to the peak of physical fitness.

I was introduced to a wrestler named Rex Casey, whom I can only describe as a type of modern-style cage fighter, as he combined boxing with wrestling. Rex invited me to travel Europe with him, fighting whatever opposition was put in front of us. I think the last guy to try to conquer Europe in a land war was Adolf Hitler, and we all know what happened to him. Nevertheless, Rex and I set off for France in his van, which had a sign in the back, scribbled in poor French, that read something like, 'Two English fighters, will take on any men anywhere for cash.' After arriving in France, we parked up in industrial areas, outside pubs around docks and anywhere else that we thought we might find willing opponents. Rex had been doing this for several years and had numerous contacts in cities throughout Europe, which ensured we were fighting at least eight or ten times per week. We met a fellow fighter from Denmark who put us in touch with an unlicensed promoter in Copenhagen. Unlike the unlicensed bouts in which I had fought in the UK, these had no rules whatsoever, so fighters could kick, head-butt and bite. I suffered a broken arm and cheekbone in a cage fight in Copenhagen and a broken hand in Frankfurt, Germany, but apart from that I remained relatively unscathed.

I earned good money fighting in Europe, so when I returned to England I placed an advert in a newspaper offering a £10,000 bet against any man who thought he could fight and defeat me. I was lunging a horse in a field within hours of the newspaper being published when Simey Doherty (a relative of Paddy Doherty) pulled up next to me in a Shogun.

'Is that you in the newspaper?' Simey asked.

'It is, yes.'

'Good, because I've brought Willy McGinley to fight you,' Simey said.

I didn't know if McGinley could fight, so, rather than let him prepare himself, I spun around and landed a perfect right hook under his chin as he stepped out of the Shogun. McGinley stumbled, fell and remained motionless face down on the ground. I picked up the lunging rein as if nothing had happened and carried on training the horse. 'That's £10,000 you owe me, Simey,' I said nonchalantly. I then told a lad who had been helping me with the horses to drive the Shogun to my house before informing Simey that it wouldn't be returned until his debt was paid.

Nobody else responded to my advertisement, but I did manage to arrange a few unlicensed bouts. I fought Jerry Golden, an ex-professional light heavyweight boxer, at a working men's club in Wigan and stopped him in two rounds. I also fought Tony Best, a former super middleweight, at Duckingfield Town Hall and stopped him in five rounds.

In the sport of unlicensed fighting, I felt I had found a pastime that suited my age and dwindling capabilities. Most of the fighters in the unlicensed bouts at that time were about my age and were hampered by the same ageing process. I felt that I could fight on for a couple more years so long as I remained injury free. After that, I thought I would like to try my hand at promoting, managing or training boxers.

In order to set the wheels in motion for my future plans, I got in touch with Kevin Kinsella from north London. During the '70s and '80s, Kinsella promoted shows with the likes of Shirley Bassey and Petula Clark; he also promoted several boxers, including me. It was agreed that Kevin would form two companies, the British Boxing Federation and the European Boxing Federation, so that we could train and manage fighters and promote lucrative shows in the future.

For many years, the British Boxing Board of Control governed the sport without hindrance or interference from anybody. The last bare-knuckle fight on English soil to attract major and widespread public interest took place at Farnborough, Hampshire, in 1860, when the undisputed champion of England, Tom Sayers, and the American champion John Carmel Heenan battered each other into oblivion in 2 hours and 27 minutes. It was a somewhat bizarre and brutal fight. Heenan appeared to be winning, but the crowd rallied to Sayers' assistance by invading the ring. When order was finally restored, a devastating blow from Heenan fractured Sayers' right arm, but still he boxed on. Police officers tried to stop the fight in the 36th round, but once more spectators spilled into the ring. The boxers fought six more rounds before it was finally declared a draw. Both fighters were awarded commemorative belts, and a public collection raised more than £3,000 for Sayers, given on condition that he never entered the ring again. Seven years later, under the patronage of the 9th Marquess of Queensberry, a Cambridge undergraduate drew up a boxing code that included the obligatory use of gloves.

More than 100 years later, cockney villain Roy 'Pretty Boy' Shaw picked up where Sayers and Heenan had left off, putting unlicensed fights back in the public arena. Shaw defeated numerous contenders from the Travelling community at Barnet Fair and was eventually challenged by a formidable fighter called Donny 'The Bull' Adams. Shaw's close friend was a notorious villain named Joey Pyle, and he saw the fight as nothing more than a huge money-making opportunity. Adams was a Traveller, so he would receive massive support from his community; Shaw was legendary in the East End of London and so he too would have huge support. Traditionally, unlicensed fights had taken place at fairs, Travellers' sites, pub car parks or scrap-metal yards. Pyle felt that the Adams v. Shaw fight would generate so much interest that it should be staged in a larger, more lucrative arena, like a professional event.

He hired a large field from a farmer and erected beer tents and a ring. Pony racing was organised, along with various other forms of entertainment. For a mere ten pounds, customers were guaranteed an entire day of fun. However, the chief constable of Essex Police had other plans. Ten days before the event, with hundreds of tickets already sold, he contacted Pyle and said that there was no way the fight was going to be allowed to take place. Despite his best efforts to inform ticket holders, Pyle was unable to contact everybody. On the day of the event, the field was filled with disgruntled Travellers baying for Joe Pyle's blood. 'We have been conned,' they told the television news crews that had flocked to the scene. 'Roy Shaw and his cronies haven't heard the end of this.'

Initially, Pyle was concerned, but then he realised that the publicity would create more interest in the fight. More interest meant more money, and that appealed to him. Over the next few days and weeks, Pyle tried in vain to put the fight on, but he was told it couldn't go ahead unless it was governed by the British Boxing Board of Control. Pyle conceded that the event appeared to have hit a brick wall. There was no way Adams and Shaw were going to be granted licences to box. Both were considered to be too old, and both had criminal convictions.

The hype surrounding the fight continued to grow in the media, so the police decided to take some pre-emptive action in the hope it would end all the speculation about it ever taking place. They arrested Adams and Shaw and charged them with breach of the peace. Unwittingly, the police had set in motion a chain of events that would decriminalise unlicensed fighting. When the men appeared in court, Adams told the magistrate, 'You cannot stop me and Shaw having this fight. It might take place in a park, where innocent people might get hurt, but it will take place. We had hoped that by staging it in a ring, we might be able to make it safer, but now that has been denied to us.' When Shaw was asked if he had anything to say, he told the magistrate that in borstal he had been advised to sort his differences out with people in the ring rather than in the street. 'It was,' Shaw said, 'the way I preferred to resolve disputes.' The prosecution said that, despite the men's apparent willingness to fight, the police had been forced to intervene because it was a criminal offence for any fighter not to wear gloves or to fight without a time limit.

The magistrate thought long and hard, referred to a pile of law books on his bench and then looked up to address the court. 'As long as the defendants wear boxing gloves, employ the services of a proper referee and moderate the fight using timed rounds, the fight, should they choose to partake in one, whether licensed or unlicensed, would not be illegal.'

Joe Pyle was ecstatic. He immediately contacted Billy Smart and secured the use of his big top circus tent, which was conveniently not in use and being stored in Windsor for the winter. The fight, if a ten-second brawl can be described as such, was a disappointing spectacle to watch, but it was a huge success for Pyle and Shaw.

The moment Donny Adams kissed the canvas, offers to fight Shaw came flooding in from across the country and unlicensed fighting once more, to the annoyance of the BBBC, became a sport the general public could enjoy.

When Kevin Kinsella formed the BBF and the EBF, there was a lot of positive publicity. I have always thought very highly of Kevin Kinsella – he was like a father figure to me – and so I was determined that our venture should succeed. I arranged to fight a bare-knuckle bout against a former sparring partner named Alex Penarski at the Midland Hotel in Manchester. We sold 450 tickets at £100 each, but two days before the fight the police stepped in and said that the fight could not take place because they had 'safety concerns'. The hotel management were not going to debate the issue with the police, so they just informed me that the event had been cancelled. It was bad enough having to give £45,000 back to people, but I had lost an additional £10,000 organising and promoting the event.

Within a few weeks, Alex and I had secured an alternative venue, the Queen Elizabeth Hall in Oldham. We sold 250 tickets, but the night before the fight the police once more stepped in and cancelled the event on the grounds of health and safety.

I began training hard for a fight that had been arranged to take place at a working men's club in Wigan in front of

600 people. My opponent was a 6 ft 6 in. heavyweight named Paul King, from Sheffield, and the winner's purse was to be £10,000. Within a few months, I was super-fit and ready to take on anybody.

Despite being four stone lighter and eight inches shorter than King, I was in no doubt that I would beat him. King had a large following that booed and jeered as I entered the ring. I prefer to do my talking with my fists, so I didn't respond. The compère that night was a good friend of mine named Foo Foo Lammar, and he fought my corner by ridiculing one or two of the more vocal Yorkshiremen.

Foo Foo, or Frank Pearson as he was called when I first met him, was a drag act who had borrowed his stage name from Hollywood actress Hedy Lamarr. Frank left school at an early age without any qualifications and began singing in pubs to earn a wage. When his father, Charlie, first saw his stage act at the Ancoats Arms, he threw a bar stool across the crowded room at him. Somebody had told Frank's father that he was singing in the pub that day, but what they had failed to mention was that he would be doing so stretched across a piano in a frock. Despite Frank's feminine side, he was a very tough man and a formidable boxer. Everybody in Manchester knew him. Sir Alex Ferguson was a friend of Foo Foo's and wrote the foreword to his book *I Am What I Am*.

The first time in my life that I ever worked as a bouncer was at Foo Foo's club in Newton Heath. I was only 17 years of age at the time and he used to pay me £10 per shift. Homosexuality was still a bit of a taboo back then, so the sight of Foo Foo prancing around in a ballgown inevitably resulted in trouble from time to time. I vividly remember one night when we stood side by side fighting half a dozen Scouse dockers whom I had refused entry to the club. As soon as the first punch was thrown, Foo Foo kicked his high heels off, gathered up his gown and flew at the opposition. One man was head-butted and fell to the ground, and he was soon joined by two others whom Foo Foo struck with devastating ferocity.

The man in my corner for the King fight was a Gypsy named Nathan McGowan. When I walked to my corner before the first bell, he asked if I wanted water or spray to cool myself down between rounds. I looked at the baying crowd, looked back at Nathan and said, 'I won't need either.' I smashed King to pieces in the first round; he suffered broken ribs and a fractured jaw before going down.

If I'd known then what I know now, I would have battered him before he left his dressing-room. It later emerged that for many years King had been raping women. In 2007, at Sheffield Crown Court, he was given three life sentences after being found guilty of raping two prostitutes and a teenager. King attempted to strangle his victims while using his mobile phone to take photographs of them. The prosecution at his trial described him as being 'devoid of humanity and conscience'. He would have been devoid of a lot more if I had been aware of his disgusting behaviour when we met.

Shortly after the King fight, I bumped into my old manager Nat Basso at a boxing show in Manchester. I was genuinely pleased to see him and he seemed pleased to see me too. I told him that I was still involved in boxing and he advised me to give up fighting and take up training. 'You're getting too old now, Wayne,' he said, 'but you should pass on the knowledge you have, because you were a talent.' I didn't think I would be given a licence to train young people because of my convictions, but Nat assured me that anything was possible.

The following week, he rang me and asked if I would meet him at the Cedar Court Hotel in Huddersfield. When

I arrived, he told me that he had arranged for me to appear in front of the BBBC to apply for my trainer's licence. I wasn't prepared, but I did as Nat asked and that afternoon I was granted my licence.

I always think that fate brought me and Nat Basso together that night in Manchester. I hadn't seen him for years and shortly afterwards he died. Because Nat was Jewish, he was buried the day after he died, as is traditional. I didn't learn of his death until three days later, so sadly I missed the funeral. I will never forget the many lessons that Nat Basso taught me in life. He was truly a great man.

ROUND TEN

Keep on Running

HAVING OBTAINED MY trainer's licence I began looking for young boxers who possessed that little extra something that might catapult them from obscurity to worldwide fame. It's a process that you can dedicate your life to without any result, or you can get lucky and find a genuine talent almost immediately. My instinct to make money and my love of those who have no fear resulted in me recruiting boxers whom I thought I'd be able to win money with in unlicensed fighting while I waited to discover a genuine title contender.

While trawling the various gymnasiums throughout the North and North-west, I met an ex-fighter named Mickey 'No Pain' Johnson. He had retired from the ring 11 years earlier after suffering a broken hand during a bout. After watching Mickey train, I thought that he possessed a knockout punch but had no idea how to defend himself. Mickey was a single parent with two sons. He had recently decided to return to boxing and asked me if I could find him a few fights. I managed to arrange an unlicensed bout for Mickey against a fighter from Rotherham named Steve Frost.

He was three stone heavier than Mickey, powerfully built and oozed confidence. The fight took place at Northgate Working Men's Club in Mexborough. With all due respect to Mickey, he shouldn't have been in the same country as Frost, never mind the same ring. He was battered from the moment the bell rang and didn't even last the first round. Mickey's kids might have gone hungry that week, but I was forced to gorge on humble pie. I wasn't very pleased with Mickey, because I had spent a lot of time talking him through how he should tackle his opponent, but on the night he had totally disregarded my advice. Mickey had gone in all guns blazing and Frost had punished him.

A month after the fight, if it can be described as such, I was contacted by model and accomplished amateur athlete Nell McAndrew, who said she was looking for people to appear in a TV series called *Born Fighter*. The programme was to look at aspects of boxing, from those who had turned professional to those like Mickey who simply loved to fight, regardless of ability. When I told Nell about Mickey, she asked if he would be willing to have a rematch with Frost, as it would be interesting to film the pre-fight training and build-up for the programme. Without hesitation Mickey agreed, as did Frost.

When interviewed about the forthcoming bout, Frost said, 'I am twelve out of ten confident of doing what I did last time. I knocked him out in less than a minute and I will do it again.' My advice to Mickey was simple: 'Listen to me this time and you will win, because Frost hasn't got a boxing brain.'

On the night of the fight, we were greeted by a very hostile crowd in Frost's local working men's club. The crowd booed and jeered as we walked to the ring. I told Mickey to ignore the TV cameras and the abuse and stay focused on whatever I had to say.

I told him: 'Keep Frost away from you. I've studied him, and when he throws a punch he drops his guard. You have one chance and one chance only. When he throws a

190

right-hander, you have to move your head, step towards him and throw the biggest left hook you have ever thrown.'

When the bell rang to signal the first round, Mickey began retreating from his opponent. This made Frost advance towards him. Then when Frost threw a right hook, Mickey did exactly what I had told him and, just 38 seconds into the bout, knocked him out. Frost remained on the canvas for some time and when he got to his feet his legs were like rubber. To everybody's surprise, the referee allowed Frost to continue boxing, but in less than ten seconds he had collapsed again and his corner had thrown the towel in. It was a great night for Mickey and his two sons, and one I think they must have relived many times watching Nell McAndrew's programme on video.

Away from the ring I was still running the scrap-metal yards and trying to earn money whenever an opportunity arose. Because of the rising price of aluminium, I decided to look into the possibility of processing metal in my yard. I formed a company called Manchester Reclamation and began melting down aluminium in an old chimney. However, the yard was too small, so I began looking for alternative premises. There was an old hat-making factory in nearby Denton and I managed to rent two 5,000-square-metre units from the owner on a six-month lease. I installed two furnaces and a machine that crushed car engines. I then approached every scrap dealer within a 25-mile radius and offered them a very high rate for scrap engines, gearboxes and anything else that contained aluminium. When the scrap was delivered to the yard, it was crushed and melted into ingots. Within a very short period of time, I had amassed several hundred tonnes of the precious metal.

The companies that had delivered the scrap had insisted that all invoices should be paid within 28 days, but I had no intention of giving any of them anything. After they sent several reminders regarding payment, they resorted to ringing me constantly, but I just gave them excuses and promises that I had no intention of fulfilling. Within six months of starting the company, I was able to afford a fleet of brand-new vehicles, in which I had people scouring the North-west collecting more scrap metal.

I knew it was only a matter of time before things came to a head, so I talked a lad named Mick Smythe into fronting another company in Salford called Top Spec Alloys. I hired a suitable yard in Mick's name, registered the company in his name and moved the machinery, furnaces and stock from Manchester Reclamation down to Salford. In order to distance myself from the new company and still have a legitimate income, I set up Barker Racing Stables at a farm called Croft End in Bardsley. I purchased several horses and would train them every day. To the outside world, I appeared to be a respectable person who was hard at work trying to break into the horse-racing world.

All of the businesses I had immersed myself in were doing well, but my home life was even better. Julie fell pregnant for a second time and suggested that we should get married. To be perfectly honest, I couldn't see the point, as we were living together anyway, but Julie would not let up and eventually I agreed. On the morning that we were due to be wed, I got up for work as usual at five and climbed into my car. 'What do you think you're doing? We're supposed to be getting married today,' Julie shouted through the passenger window. I switched the car engine off and wound the window down. 'I know we're getting married, but that's this afternoon. I still have time to go to work. I'll see you later,' I said, before driving away. I started up the furnaces at the yard, opened up the gates and was unloading scrap from customers' vehicles by 6 a.m. At lunchtime, I went home, showered, changed and was at the registry office by

2 p.m. There I accosted two strangers to act as our witnesses, we married and I was back at work by 3.30 p.m. Julie accused me of being cold, uncaring and unromantic, so to make amends I took her out on the town that night.

I soon discovered that there was good money to be made from horses. Every month, I advertised what is known as a dispersal sale in the *Manchester Evening News*. Horse lovers from all over the North-west and beyond would arrive en masse and purchase ex-racehorses and showjumpers for three or four times the price that I had paid for them. The business was well received in the equestrian community, so much so that I had to rent larger premises, the Bluebell Stables in Knutsford, Cheshire.

I am not the sort of man who saves his money. As soon as I had earned it, I was spending it, on clothes, cars and partying hard. Inevitably, things started to go wrong. Several companies began court proceedings against me for money that they were owed, and Julie and I began to argue. I can say now that she was right to complain. The late nights, the nights I never came home and, of course, my ability to waste money all caused Julie hurt. At the time, I was enjoying myself and convinced beyond doubt that I had done no wrong. Cracks began to appear in our marriage and before too long it was apparent that we did not have a future together.

I used to buy the feed for my horses from a man named Frank Cole. The first time I met Frank was on an extremely cold winter's morning. I pulled up in his yard in my Range Rover dressed in a thick woollen jumper and a wax coat, and Frank approached me wearing short trousers and a vest. From that moment on, I always thought that Frank was slightly insane, but, despite his unconventional manner, we got on well.

He always delivered the feed to the stables on time, but

approximately three months after I got to know him Frank failed to show and I ran out of horse feed. I decided that I would go down to his yard and pick up a few bales of feed, which would see me through until he was able to make the delivery. As I drove into his yard, a girl aged about 17 walked out of Frank's house. I will never forget how she looked. She had jodhpurs and an emerald green jumper on, and long, curly red hair down her back. I said to my friend, 'I have just got to have that.' He laughed and said I had no chance, as she was way out of my league. I took out a £50 note and bet my friend that I would indeed one day win her over. I got out of my vehicle and called the girl over. I asked her who she was and explained that I had come to pick up some horse feed. 'I'll get the feed for you. My name is Sharon. Frank is my father,' she replied. I chatted to Sharon for some time, gave her my number and assured her that we would meet again. Over the next few weeks, Sharon would visit my stables, exercise horses for me and generally help out. One day, Sharon suggested that we go out for a drink. I agreed, of course, and that night I won my £50 bet.

Not only did my marriage hit rock bottom when I began an affair with Sharon, so too did my finances. In an effort to impress my teenage mistress, I was taking her to stay at top-class hotels every weekend, both in Britain and abroad. I also provided her with top-of-the-range vehicles to drive and lavished her with expensive gifts. Before I knew it, I didn't even have enough money to pay my mortgage.

One afternoon, a man from the Inland Revenue arrived at the stables, clipboard in hand. I was elsewhere, fortunately, but he asked Sharon a series of questions concerning the purchase and sale of horses, which he claimed had made me thousands of pounds in profit. Acting naive, Sharon told the man that she was merely a hired hand who mucked out and fed the animals; she said she knew nothing of my dealings whatsoever. The tax inspector left but vowed to return. Over the next few days, I sold all of the horses, pocketed more than £30,000 in cash and walked away.

Most families could manage to live comfortably on £30,000 per year back then, but it only lasted me a few weeks. I purchased a car, bought Sharon clothes and blew the rest travelling, dining out at top-class restaurants and staying in luxury hotels. While I was away enjoying myself, back home my family were suffering. Julie was finding it hard to make ends meet; she didn't even have enough money to pay the mortgage. When I returned home broke, there were several heated rows and I was forced to sell my car.

I then went directly to the building society in order to pay the outstanding instalments on the mortgage. It didn't feel right handing over nearly £3,000, but it was a case of doing so or my family becoming homeless. Banks and building societies back then were much friendlier places than they are today. There weren't any security screens, hi-tech alarms or even CCTV. When I handed my not-so-hard-earned cash over, I noticed that the cashier put it into a small safe on the floor near her desk. I decided there and then that I would be back later that night to reclaim it.

I recruited two young Travellers for the task, and as darkness fell they kicked open the rear door of the building society. They picked up the locked safe, threw it into the back of my van and we all made our getaway. I paid the lads £100 each before dropping them home, and then I set about cutting the back of the safe off. As well as recovering my mortgage money, I had an additional £2,500 in cash and a large bundle of blank banker's drafts. To be honest, I didn't have a clue what they were, but the following day I made enquiries and learned that I was now in possession of some extremely valuable paperwork.

When somebody is given a normal cheque, they present

it at their bank and if the person or organisation that produced the cheque has sufficient funds in their account it is honoured. Banker's drafts are slightly different. If somebody asks a bank or a building society for a banker's draft, the amount is taken from their account and paid to the bank or building society before the draft is handed over. Because the funds of a banker's draft have already been transferred, they are proven to be available and the draft will therefore be guaranteed to be honoured when presented to a private individual, business or bank.

In order to test the validity of the drafts I had acquired, I telephoned a man from Stockport who was advertising a second-hand vehicle in *Auto Trader* for £5,000. He agreed to pick me up at Stockport train station and took me for a test drive, after which we shook hands on a deal. I asked him how he wanted paying and he replied, 'Cash or preferably a banker's draft.' The next morning, I arrived at his home in a taxi, handed him a banker's draft for £4,750 and left shortly afterwards in his car. The following night, the vehicle was sold at an auction for £4,000.

For the next few days, I sat at home scouring *Auto Trader* for high-value second-hand cars. I would ring the owner and pretend I was a car dealer. Once I had been assured that the vehicle was as described (I didn't want to be ripped off), I would agree a price, agree to pay by banker's draft and then arrange to have a driver drop the banker's draft off and pick up the car.

The eighth or ninth car that I acquired using the stolen banker's drafts was a wide-bodied Porsche 944 Turbo from a dealership in Newport. On my way home, I decided to do a bit of showing off and visit my uncle Jimmy in North Wales. I was hurtling along the Sealand bypass at approximately 125 mph when I literally took off on a humpbacked bridge. As the car hit the road, a shower of sparks flashed in front of me and I thought I was going to crash. Fear was replaced by relief as the car steadied and I regained control.

Unfortunately, a police patrol car was parked in a lay-by and an officer had witnessed my reckless driving. As soon as the blue lights and siren were activated on the police vehicle, I pulled over and buried my face in my hands.

I could sense the police officer standing next to my open window, so I said, 'I am so sorry. I've just purchased this car and I'm not used to the speed. It felt like I was doing 50 or 60 mph, but it must have been nearer 70 mph.'

'Try 120 or 130 mph and you're close,' the officer replied sarcastically.

I was asked to produce my documents and step out of the car. After checking my identity and the documentation, the officer lectured me on the dangers of speeding before allowing me to drive away.

Three days later, I obtained a limited-edition 75th anniversary Rolls-Royce Silver Shadow with a £25,000 banker's draft. It was a beautiful car, oyster and gold in colour, gold-plated dashboard, the works. I sold this vehicle shortly afterwards for £20,000 cash to Paddy Doherty's uncle Simey, who ran the Duchy Road Travellers' site in Salford. Simey had then taken it to a car dealer named Ashley, who had premises on Milton Road in Manchester. Ashley asked Simey how much he wanted for the vehicle and he had replied £22,000. Being a legitimate and honest businessman, Ashley had telephoned the previous owner of the Rolls-Royce and asked if he had recently sold the vehicle and if so for how much. When Ashley put the phone down, he told Simey that he had no interest in the vehicle, as the previous owner had raised concerns about the banker's draft he had received and the matter was now being investigated by the police. It's fair to say that Simey was not happy with me and the car was parked back on my drive within the hour.

If the police were investigating the Rolls-Royce sale, I knew I would have to get rid of the Porsche as soon as possible, so I offered it to a car dealer named Bobby Irwin. He took the vehicle to a Toyota dealership, where he was offered cash and a Toyota Supra in exchange. I pocketed £4,000 in cash, sold the Toyota privately for £14,000 and gave Bobby £1,000 for his troubles.

Later that day, I was at home talking to a guy named Frankie Crawford when I heard a noise at the back gate. I looked at Frankie, but he didn't appear to have heard anything. 'One moment, I just need to check something,' I said as I rose to my feet. I walked out into the garden and looked over the wall. Two police officers were standing at the back gate and one of them ordered me to unlock it. 'No problem, officer. I'll just go and get the key,' I lied.

I walked back into the lounge, past Frankie and into the kitchen. Looking out the front window, I could see a group of policemen peering into the Rolls-Royce, which was still parked on my drive. Walking back into the lounge, I gathered up some paperwork and burnt it in the fireplace.

'What's going on, Wayne?' Frankie asked.

'We're surrounded, mate. Any minute now we're going to be nicked,' I replied.

I took the SIM cards out of my phone and Frankie's and hid them, and then I opened the front door.

DS Hulse, who had investigated me previously for the stolen vehicles from Mitchell's Self Drive, informed me that I was under arrest. Frankie and I were taken to Platt Lane police station in Moss Side and locked in separate cells until the following morning.

When my solicitor arrived shortly after 9 a.m., I was taken to an interview room where DS Hulse was waiting. I explained that I had purchased the Rolls-Royce from a man named Charles Marion. Of course, I had never met anybody by that name; Charles Marion Russell was an artist who used to paint cowboys, Indians and landscapes. I had recently seen a print of one of his paintings hanging in a Blackpool restaurant. His name had stuck in my mind and I just blurted it out to the police. When asked how I had paid Marion, I replied, 'Cash.' The police were well aware that I was responsible for the fraud, but I never used to physically hand over the drafts or pick up the cars myself, so they couldn't prove it.

Despite the lack of evidence, Crawford and I were charged with obtaining goods by deception and bailed to appear at court at a later date. It looked as if I would have to stop using the banker's drafts for a while, so I began looking elsewhere for an income.

I became aware of a large disused textile mill that was for sale in Gibbon Street, Manchester. The area was predominantly industrial and these days sits in the shadow of Manchester City Football Club's Etihad Stadium. When I made enquiries about purchasing the mill, I was told that the asking price was £110,000. I didn't have that sort of cash, so I teamed up with a guy whom I'll call Martin and together we talked two men, whom I'll refer to as Simpson and Davies, into forming a consortium. I lied about having been promised planning permission to build numerous luxury flats and houses on the site, so they invested £10,000 each, which I assured them would reap huge returns.

I had £10,000 of my own money to add to the £20,000, but I still needed to find an additional £80,000 to purchase the mill. I approached various financial advisers who assured me that they would be able to secure loans for me, but, after they'd taken a consultancy fee, what they promised failed to materialise. Confident that I was going to get the £80,000 one way or another, I had proceeded with the purchase and signed the sales agreement forms. When the estate agent began ringing me to enquire about why the cash hadn't been transferred into their account, I made excuse after excuse until eventually I stopped answering their calls.

I had a brand-new Escort van sign-written with the name Barclay Demolition and Redevelopment on the side and went to work stripping the mill roof. The old slates and lead were valuable, and I hoped they would go some way to getting the additional £80,000 that was needed.

Time was running out for me, so I spoke to another financial adviser about a loan. He too assured me that it wouldn't be a problem. Because I had been let down previously, I followed the financial adviser and discovered that he lived in a big house in Cheshire. Every night, the financial adviser would arrive home, park his vehicle in his drive, walk into his home and then emerge moments later with his Dobermann. He would then enjoy a 30-minute walk in the park. Martin and I waited outside the man's home one evening. When he emerged with his dog, Martin leapt out at him from a bush. As the man jumped back, Martin grabbed the animal and severed its head with a machete. I drove full speed towards Martin and pulled up inches from him and the man, who had begun to scream. Martin threw the headless dog's corpse into the back of my van and then threw the terrified man into the door. 'At ten o'clock tomorrow morning, we need £80,000 to be in the estate agent's account. Do you understand?' Martin said. Pleading for his life, the man stared at his Dobermann's head, which was still on the drive, and nodded furiously. 'It will be, I promise. Just please don't hurt me,' he begged. Martin picked up the dog's head, volleyed it into the back of the van and we then drove away. The following morning, the money had been transferred into the account and I owned the mill.

Within a month, Manchester City Council had given me a written offer of £3 million in stage payments for the site.

At that time, Manchester was preparing to bid for the Olympic Games to be staged in the city, and that whole area had been earmarked for sporting venues. The bid failed, but in later years a velodrome was built on the site of the mill for the 2002 Commonwealth Games.

As soon as the documents were in my possession, I bounded into a branch of NatWest and told the manager that my name was John Barclay and I wanted to open an account in the name of Barclay Demolition and Redevelopment. After I had shown him details of the mill and the letter from the council, I left with a new account in a false name and an unsecured £90,000 overdraft.

Obtaining machinery and paying men to demolish the mill proved to be more expensive than purchasing it. I therefore needed to increase the £90,000 overdraft. I paid any money I had into the account and withdrew various amounts over the following weeks in order to give the impression that the business was ticking over. After a few months, I would be able to approach the bank manager, ask for a £150,000 overdraft, withdraw it in stages and keep the lot.

In the meantime, I needed cash to keep the mill project afloat. I was approached by a Traveller from North Wales named Rennie Hamer, who said he wanted to purchase a brand-new Mercedes 300 diesel estate car. In the past, Rennie had sold at least 20 of the stolen cars I had obtained using banker's drafts, so I agreed to help him on the condition that he would assist me. Because I was on bail for fraud, I had hidden what was left of the stolen banker's drafts. It seemed pointless leaving them to go to waste when I needed money, though, so I began looking through *Auto Trader* for suitable victims.

I soon found a guy in Stoke-on-Trent who was selling a Mercedes SL for £12,000. I rang him up, agreed the price and then sent a lad down with a banker's draft to collect the car. Everything went smoothly and I sold the vehicle the same day for £8,000. I then found a guy in Dunstable who was selling the type of vehicle that Rennie was looking for, so I rang him up. The man said he wanted £24,000 for the car, but I talked him into selling it for £23,000. I told him that I would send a representative from my company down to collect the vehicle and asked if he would be kind enough to collect him from the train station at 11 a.m. the following day. The man agreed and insisted he be paid by banker's draft, as he foolishly believed that they were secure.

The following morning, I drove to Bedfordshire with another man. At 10 a.m., I dropped my accomplice off at Dunstable train station and he purchased a platform ticket. When a train pulled into the station at 11 a.m., my associate waited for a couple of minutes, then walked through the ticket barrier with passengers who had just alighted from the train. He made a point of looking around him until the guy who was waiting to meet him beeped his horn. He then tossed his platform ticket into a bin and climbed into the waiting car. I followed them back to the man's house and parked in a nearby street. Approximately 30 minutes later, I saw my associate drive past me in the Mercedes and so I followed him.

When we were on the motorway, we pulled into a service station, swapped vehicles and then I drove to the Gypsy site in North Wales where Rennie was staying. When I pulled up outside his trailer, Rennie held his head in his hands and began saying, 'No, you should never have brought that here.' I immediately thought he was trying to somehow con me, so I said, 'No problem. I'll sell it to somebody else.' Rennie said that he wanted the car but he didn't want it being seen outside his trailer, so we agreed to meet up in Manchester the following day.

That night, I parked the vehicle outside my house and

went to bed. Unbeknown to me, I was under surveillance by Greater Manchester Police. A very good friend of mine named Robert Chic Thompson had recently received a 12-year term of imprisonment for armed robbery. He had feigned an illness in prison, which resulted in him being rushed to the Hope Hospital, where Sharon was working as a trainee nurse. Moments after the ambulance arrived at the accident and emergency department, Chic leapt off his stretcher and ran down the street. The police somehow discovered that I regularly visited the Hope Hospital and concluded that I must have played some sort of role in Chic's escape. They then assumed that he would get in touch with me and so placed me under surveillance in the hope of catching him.

As soon as I had parked outside my home, the officers watching me had checked the registration of the vehicle. They were informed that the registered keeper was a chief inspector at Bedfordshire police. Alarm bells began to ring, so Greater Manchester Police contacted the officer in Bedfordshire and asked him where his car was. He explained that he had sold it earlier that day and had been paid by banker's draft.

The following morning, Rennie arrived at my house and gave me £18,000 in cash for the Mercedes. I took £1,000 out for the driver who had accompanied me to pick up the car, I gave £15,000 to Julie to put in the bank and I put the remaining £2,000 in my pocket. Moments later, Julie walked out of the house with the £15,000 in her bag. After having a cup of tea, Rennie and I walked out and got into the Mercedes. Seemingly from nowhere, we were surrounded by at least 15 officers who were all shouting and demanding that we get out of the vehicle. When we did so, my old adversary DS Hulse was standing directly in front of me.

'Now then, Wayne, what's the story this morning?' he said.

'I'm on my way to the auction to buy a car. Why, what's up with you?' I asked.

DS Hulse asked who owned the vehicle and, not being the type to tell lies, I looked at Rennie and said, 'That man there.'

DS Hulse arrested Rennie on suspicion of obtaining property by deception and placed him in the back of a police van. Rennie was taken away and the police began a search of my home but found nothing of significance.

I was then taken to Whitefield police station near Bury and interviewed under caution. I had been on bail for five months awaiting trial for obtaining property by deception, but when I was charged a second time for the same offence DS Hulse said he wasn't going to bail me as he feared I would abscond.

When the police searched Rennie's trailer, they found £50,000 in a suitcase and several brand-new vehicles nearby that he claimed he had no knowledge of. Unfortunately for Rennie, his fingerprints were all over the interiors of the cars, so he too was charged and denied bail.

The following morning, we both appeared in court and the prosecution asked the magistrates to remand us both in custody. Our respective solicitors argued that we had not yet been convicted of any offence and therefore we should not lose our liberty. Rennie Hamer's bail application was refused and he was sent to HMP Strangeways to await trial. I, on the other hand, was granted bail.

While I had been in custody, certain people had assumed that I wasn't going to get out in the near future and had imagined that they could take over the mill project. I instructed Sharon to go to the office at the mill and retrieve £10,000 that I had left in the safe. When she was leaving the office with the money, Simpson, who had invested £10,000 in the project, began shouting at her. He demanded to know what Sharon was up to and who had given her the authority to remove money from the safe. Sharon was still a teenager and not used to being shouted at in that manner, so she burst out crying and ran out of the door. She then rang my father who immediately drove down to the Mill and offered to fight Simpson. Words were exchanged, but the dispute ended without any physical violence. On the day I was released from police custody, my father told me what had happened.

As I drove towards the mill, I could feel my temper rising. Simpson was bigger than me and I knew he was going to be no pushover. 'Get out in this yard and fight me,' I shouted at him through the office window when I arrived. Simpson came out with his hands up and said he didn't want any trouble. I continued shouting at him in the hope that I could provoke him into fighting me, but he wasn't having any of it. 'You only put £10,000 into this project. Who the fuck do you think you are? If you ever talk to anybody I know like that again, I will smash you all over the street,' I said as I walked back towards my car.

Prior to being arrested, I had acquired a Range Rover, which I had given to my father. He drove into the mill just as I was about to leave, and I asked him if I could borrow it for the evening, as I wanted to take Sharon out. 'No problem. You get in here and I'll drive your car,' my father replied. A few minutes later, we both drove into one of my scrapyards and parked. As we were getting out of our vehicles, several police cars raced into the yard and blocked the entrance.

'What's your name?' one of the officers asked.

'Barry Barker,' I replied.

'And yours?'

'Eric Barker,' my father replied.

We were then asked who owned the Range Rover and my

father said that he did. The officer began to read my father his rights, as he had been placed under arrest on suspicion of fraudulently obtaining the Range Rover. I started to walk away. 'Where do you think you're going?' the officer called out. I told him that I had to put the guard dogs away, as they could be dangerous with strangers. The truth was I had no intention of being locked up on the very day that I had been released from custody.

I disappeared behind a Portakabin, scaled the yard fence, dropped into the street and began to run. When I reached a main road, I managed to flag down a taxi and escape from the area. Over the next few days, I withdrew £49,000 from the Allied Irish Bank and what was left of my NatWest overdraft, which was £35,000. Sharon and I then left Manchester and moved to Anglesey in North Wales.

ROUND ELEVEN

I Don't Know Why You Say Hello, I Say Goodbye

SHORTLY AFTER SHARON and I arrived in Anglesey, Julie informed me that she was seeking a divorce, as our marriage had now ended. I am not sure how I really felt, to be honest.

This may sound ridiculous to most people, but I have no concept of growing old. I still feel the same way now as I did when I was 16, 18 or 21 years of age. I am 52 at the time of writing this, and if I look at a 40-year-old woman I can't help but think she looks like my mother. Uncaring, selfish, immature – I am probably guilty of being all three and more, but that's the way I was made and that's the way I am.

I told Julie she could have a divorce, but deep inside it did make me extremely unhappy. Had I not been on the run, had I been at liberty to live with Julie and our children, I might well have reached a different conclusion. Despite the pending divorce, Julie and I remained friends, and it was me she would turn to in times of trouble.

One weekend, my father arrived in Anglesey with Julie, our children and three quad bikes. It was a beautiful day, so we all went to the beach. My eldest son, James, was racing his quad bike along the sand and disturbed a guy who was sunbathing. He got upset and began shouting at me to keep my children under control. Five minutes later, we were heading home and the man with no manners was back sunbathing on the beach – only this time he was unconscious.

If the police wish to arrest you in Anglesey, they know that you can only leave the island via the Menai Bridge, so they rarely bother scouring the streets for you. I knew this, and I also knew that when the guy whom I had knocked out with a right hook came around on the beach he would be contacting the police. There is another way of leaving Anglesey: you can catch the ferry from Holyhead to Dublin. I told Sharon to pack her belongings, kissed my children goodbye and within the hour had boarded a ship for Ireland.

I had approximately £100,000 with me, so I wasn't in any rush to get involved in any schemes or crimes. We rented a house in a town called Bray, 13 miles south of Dublin in County Wicklow. It's a beautiful area that is known as the gateway to the garden of Ireland. For the first few weeks, Sharon and I relaxed and tried to forget the problems that I had left back in England. Then, a month after we'd arrived in Ireland, Sharon announced that she had fallen pregnant. I was naturally happy, but I also knew that I would have to provide for the child, so I started to look for ways to make money.

I knew a few guys in Dublin from the days when I used to fight at Smithfield Market for the Travellers. Through them, I started importing Volkswagen Jettas. At that time, a VW Jetta cost about £8,000 in the UK; in Ireland it was nearer £15,000. If you wanted to import one via the UK, you had to pay an additional 70 per cent of the cost of the car in duty (so if a vehicle cost £10,000 in the UK, you had to pay £17,000 to buy and import it into Ireland), minus 10 per cent for every year that it had been on the road. For some reason, the same rule did not apply to vehicles purchased in Japan, so I formed a company called Anglo-Irish Imports and began importing VW Jettas from Japan. I sold them to taxi firms based in O'Connell Street and soon I was unable to meet the demand. I therefore began buying stolen Jettas registered in Ireland or hiring them, changing the number plates and selling them as legitimate vehicles.

One afternoon, I was drinking in a bar in Smithfield Market when a Toyota HiAce van pulled up outside. The doors opened and six burly men got out. They walked straight up to me, hauled me to my feet and threw me into the bar wall.

'Hold on here, lads. What's the problem?' I asked.

'You're the fucking problem. You've ripped the wrong people off,' one of them said as he aimed a handgun at my head.

I pointed out to the irate Irishman that if he pulled the trigger nobody would get anything. 'I would much rather we sit down and sort this out,' I reasoned.

I was put in the back of the van and driven to my office. Once inside, I appealed for the men to be rational. 'Do I know you? No. I am over here grafting. Have a word with yourself. You would be doing the same, right? Come on, lads. Let's have no fucking dramas.'

My direct approach appeared to be working, as the men began to relax. I was asked how I proposed to sort the 'misunderstanding' out, so I offered to replace the VW Jetta I'd sold them – which the police now had – with a fairly decent BMW 316. The men looked at one another and then nodded in agreement.

'You cannot come to Dublin and think you can rip people off. If you're still here next month, your car pitch and all of the cars on it will be petrol-bombed,' one of the men said. I didn't reply, and so they got back into their van and left.

Crime in Ireland is not always dealt with by the police.

If the IRA are made aware of a drug dealer, burglar or any other type of criminal operating within a community, he may be warned, ordered to leave Ireland or shot. It's not like dealing with the legitimate authorities; people are tried, convicted and often sentenced to death within minutes of being dragged off the street and beaten on the word of an informant. Because the IRA instil so much fear into members of the Irish criminal fraternity, it has been known for non-members to use their name. I have no idea who the guys who kidnapped me were. They may well have been IRA men, but it's just as likely that they were simply disgruntled customers intent on securing what they had paid for. I certainly wasn't going to hang around to find out. I concluded that it was time for me to leave Ireland. I sold all the remaining vehicles I had to a dealer I knew for cost price and caught the ferry home that night.

Sharon and I no longer had a home in England or Wales, so I headed to my cousin's house in Kinmel Bay, near Rhyl. When my cousin opened the door to me, he looked shocked. 'I don't believe this. You arrive here today of all days?' he said. I asked him what he meant and he explained that several people had been convicted of obtaining property by deception in relation to my stolen banker's drafts. 'My father and Rennie Hamer both got 12 months' imprisonment, and believe it or not I am meeting them today,' he said.

My cousin explained that there had recently been a riot in HMP Strangeways and prisoners were being moved to different locations throughout the country. Because my uncle Jimmy and Rennie were nearing the end of their sentences, they were being moved to an open prison and had been granted permission to travel without an escort by rail. 'They have to change trains at Preston and I'm going to meet them,' my cousin said.

Later that day, I met my uncle Jimmy and Rennie in the

restaurant at Preston station. It's fair to say that they didn't look too pleased to see me. I had trusted a man named Stuart from Manchester with most of the face-to-face banker's draft transactions. I used to hammer out the deals on the phone, but it was generally Stuart, acting as my driver, who would hand the drafts over to our victims and drive the vehicles away. According to Jimmy and Rennie, Stuart had told the police everything, and so the chances of me evading justice were at best slim.

After leaving Preston, I dropped Sharon off at her father's home in Manchester and went to visit my mother. I changed cars there and asked my brother-in-law if he would drive me to the Woodhouse Gardens pub, where I knew Julie would be working. Our divorce had not yet been finalised and I needed to speak to her about a few matters and arrange to see my children.

When my brother-in-law reached a junction on Ashton Road, he indicated to turn right, but I sensed something was wrong and told him to turn left. As he did so, I looked in the rear-view mirror to see if we were being followed, but the road was empty. I told my brother-in-law to take various diversions until we eventually arrived at the pub. I walked into the lounge alone and was immediately grabbed by half a dozen plain-clothes police officers.

The following morning, I appeared in court and was remanded in custody to await trial. The rioting at HMP Strangeways had sparked a series of disturbances in prisons across England, Scotland and Wales. Because of the chronic overcrowding this caused, new inmates were being kept in police-station cells. Within a three-week period, I was moved from Goole to West Bromwich and finally to Bridewell police station in Liverpool.

Bridewell is without doubt the worst place that I have ever had the misfortune to set foot in. Built in Victorian times, it was essentially a three-storey jail rather than an orthodox police station. Verbal and physical abuse dished out by overzealous police officers was a daily occurrence. I had the audacity to complain that I had been ripped off when purchasing biscuits from the canteen and was sent to my cell 'to reflect'. As soon as I had closed the door behind me and sat on my bed, the door burst open and I was attacked by baton-wielding officers. While lying on the floor, I was then beaten about the head and body with knotted towels that had been soaked in water for maximum effect. I hated every moment that I was forced to spend in that dreadful place. When Sharon came to visit me, I told her to contact my solicitor and tell him to get me out of there. A few days later, I was moved to a temporary prison in Grimsby that housed just 24 inmates.

The year after I left Bridewell, former Merseyside Police Authority chairman George Bundred branded it 'the worst jail in Britain'. Long-term remand prisoners were moved out after conditions were described as 'inhumane' by the European Committee for the Prevention of Torture. Thankfully, it was closed in 1999.

I spent three months at Grimsby before my trial started at Manchester Crown Court. I was charged with the theft of £1.7 million worth of banker's drafts, securing a pecuniary advantage (obtaining credit by fraud) and assaulting the guy on the beach in North Wales. I pleaded guilty and was sentenced to two years' imprisonment.

I have no idea what it was, but after I had been sentenced something kept telling me to study my case papers. I read and reread them for days, but I couldn't see anything untoward. Then one day, while I was on exercise, the mistake the police had made struck me like a bolt of lightning. In their efforts to resolve my case as quickly as possible, the police had mistakenly put two charges together as one offence. I had taken £90,000 off NatWest and an £80,000 loan from Hampshire Trust; however, I had faced only one charge of securing a pecuniary advantage. I had initially been arrested in September for one of the offences but had been bailed immediately afterwards pending further enquiries. Six months later, I had been rearrested and remanded in custody when the second offence came to light. When the two offences had been joined as one, the paperwork appeared to show that I had been in custody awaiting trial since September of the previous year, rather than March.

I went to the wing office and told a senior prison guard that they had miscalculated my release date. I showed him the paperwork and, after scratching his head a few times, the officer said, 'The original records would have been destroyed during the Strangeways riot, but this paperwork appears to show you're right.' The following morning, I was informed that, after time off for good behaviour and time served had been taken into account, I was to be released in just over five months. Not bad considering I had just been sentenced to serve two years.

My sons James, Wayne and Kane had moved to Basildon, Essex, with their mother while I had been on the run in Ireland. Julie had some of my personal possessions, so when I was released from prison I went to pick them up and of course spend time with my children. I returned to the North-west with not only my possessions but also James and Wayne. Kane had remained in Essex because he was very young and needed his mother.

Shortly after arriving back in Manchester, I purchased three acres of land in the village of Aston Pigott in Shropshire. There were three old buildings and two static caravans on the plot, which cost me £38,000. Aston Pigott is a very remote area, with few amenities such as schools and shops. The current population stands at 50. We moved into the caravans and I began renovating the buildings in the hope that I would get planning permission and be allowed to build a house. I started buying and selling cattle and supplying animal feed to local farmers; I was purchasing it cheaply through Sharon's father. I also set up a company called Second Time Around, which supplied reclaimed building materials and timbers. I was driving to Manchester and buying material from demolition sites, and then I would employ labourers to clean, size and cut it so that it could be sold. I made a fairly decent living out of it and soon managed to purchase a brand-new chalet. I also sent James and Wayne to a private school, St Winefride's in Shrewsbury.

Life was good for me at that time, but I couldn't help but dabble in stupid enterprises such as buying pirate videos and fake designer T-shirts and perfume. The police from Manchester, Liverpool and Shrewsbury began searching my property on a regular basis, but fortunately there was nothing illegal for them to find. One of the detectives seemed to take an unhealthy interest in me. He would arrive in my yard morning, noon and night and hang around for hours without having any sort of reasonable excuse. I knew that if I didn't do something about him he was bound to cause me problems, so one day I called him into my makeshift office.

'Give me a break, mate. I'm struggling to make an honest living here and your presence is scaring all of my customers away,' I said.

He explained that he was only doing his job and if he had his way he wouldn't be troubling me. 'It's my boss,' he said. 'He's convinced you're up to no good, so I've been told to keep a close eye on you.'

The conversation that followed resulted in me and this policeman becoming quite friendly, so on his next visit I asked him what shirt size he was. When he told me, I went out the back and returned with an Armani shirt in a presentation box. 'There you go. That's a little present for you,' I said as I offered him the box. His eyes lit up, and on his next visit he asked me if I could get any more. I was only paying £9 for the shirts, as they were fakes, but I didn't tell my fashion-conscious cop friend that. He would pay me £10 for each shirt I gave him and sell them to his colleagues for £20. Everybody was happy.

When you have a registered smallholding, you are given herd numbers for your cattle. These are just small metal tags that are usually clipped to the animal's ear for identification purposes. For several weeks after I registered my property as a smallholding, I left the bag of metal clips that I had been given in one of the sheds, as I didn't think I had any use for them. Then my criminal mentality kicked in and I began ringing around various Travellers asking if anybody had any stolen cattle that I could purchase.

Within a few hours, a Traveller named John rang me from Newcastle and we arranged to meet. A week after I had met John and told him that I would purchase as many young cattle as he could get, I received a phone call from him. 'I've got 30 cattle for you. I'll be at your yard in the morning. Make sure you have the cash,' John said. At 8 a.m. the following day, John arrived at the yard and unloaded 30 cows. He then removed their identification tags and I attached mine before paying John and bidding him farewell.

John spent so much time at my home over the next 12 months that he ended up living there. On average, he was delivering fifty stolen cattle per month, which I was then selling at various auctions for approximately three times the price I had paid for them. The average price for a one-year-old cow back then was approximately £1,200.

As well as rustling cattle, I used to sell counterfeit goods at little country fairs and markets. They were ideal venues, because they were rarely policed by trading standards officers and the customers rarely complained. One market I regularly worked was in Aberystwyth, North Wales. I had two stalls, one selling lingerie, which I worked, and another where two other lads sold snide perfume, which I had named 'Funk 'Em'. Around lunchtime one day, the lads asked me if they could have a break, so I said I would watch their stall for an hour.

Shortly after they had left, two butch women approached me who I assumed were lesbians. 'Try before you buy, ladies,' I said as I sprayed the perfume. 'It comes with a government health warning to wear below the waist and above the knee, one bottle for £15 or two for £25.' The women smelled the perfume and thanked me for the offer before walking away. A short time later, I was changing a light bulb on the lingerie stall when a man grabbed hold of me. I called out, 'What are you doing, mate?' before shoving him away.

'Who are you?' the man asked.

'Never mind who I am, who are you? You shouldn't be fucking grabbing hold of me,' I replied.

The man produced a police warrant card and informed me that I was under arrest on suspicion of selling counterfeit goods. When the two lads returned from lunch, they too were arrested and we were then all conveyed to Aberystwyth police station.

After two hours in custody, the lads were released on bail, but I was held overnight as the officers said that they needed to search my home. It was the last thing I wanted to hear, because I had 15,000 videos, 20,000 T-shirts and 10,000 sunglasses stored there that I hadn't been able to sell in the summer. I also had £280,000 worth of perfume, which I was paying £2 a bottle for at the time, and a thousand cases of fake Bollinger champagne. At the rear of my market stall, I had parked a lorry that contained an additional 100,000 bottles of perfume, and the keys to this vehicle had been found in my pocket. It suddenly dawned on me why the police had said they were going to hold me overnight: they were going to wait until the market had closed and then they would know which vehicle the keys in my pocket belonged to, as it would be the only one left in the marketplace.

I sat in my cell thinking to myself that I was in trouble here. The snide T-shirts, perfume, videos and sunglasses were no big deal, but any fake food or drink always results in a jail sentence because it could harm the consumer. Fortunately for me, when officers searched my home at 2 a.m., Sharon, who had never had any dealings with the police, was on form. They had woken her up and asked her to accompany them as they had a warrant to search our property. When they eventually located the cases of champagne, they asked Sharon who owned them. 'Every time Wayne earns a bit of money, he buys a case of champagne. He keeps threatening to bathe me in it, but he hasn't done it yet,' she replied coyly. Laughing, the officers thanked Sharon and walked out, leaving the fake champagne behind.

After I had been interviewed, I was transferred from Aberystwyth to Monkmoor police station in Shrewsbury and charged with seven offences concerning counterfeit and copyrighted material that had been found at the farm. When I was granted bail, I returned home and informed Sharon that we would soon have to move.

Shortly before being arrested, I had purchased a showjumping horse called Texan Farmer. The prizewinning horse had been a present for Sharon, who would take it to various events around the country. Sharon had a friend who used to borrow the horse to go hunting and she fell in love with it. Every time I saw this woman, she would beg me to sell the horse, but I would have to refuse and explain it was Sharon's. Driving home one afternoon, I noticed an abattoir and, without even thinking, I pulled into the car park and got out of my car. I walked into an office where half a dozen men were drinking tea.

'Now then,' I said, 'my wife had a horse delivered here yesterday. It was picked up from Aston Pigott. I need a receipt for the vet.'

'What horse was it?' one of the men enquired.

I described Sharon's horse, Texan Farmer, and after scribbling on a pad the man handed me a receipt. Fifteen minutes later, I had arrived at the vet's office, handed him the receipt and picked up a death certificate for Sharon's horse, which in reality was grazing happily in a field. The following morning, I contacted the insurance company and seven weeks later I was paid £7,000. I then took Texan Farmer to an auction in Kent, where I sold it under the name of Scholar Lass for £4,000. Sharon's friend was so distraught that I had not sold the horse to her that she rang the police and told them what I had done. I was arrested, charged and bailed once more.

When I arrived home from the police station, Sharon was in tears.

'What's the matter with you?' I asked.

'I'm pregnant, Wayne, and if you go to prison I'm going to be on my own,' Sharon sobbed.

I had no intention of returning to prison or leaving Sharon alone, so shortly afterwards I sold my businesses and moved to Glan Conwy, near Llandudno in North Wales. Because the police were looking for me, Sharon registered at a doctor's surgery in Manchester, using her parents' address so that she could attend her antenatal clinic appointments. That was a suitable arrangement for a while, but she soon grew tired of the travelling, so we rented a home in Buckley near Chester. When Sharon gave birth to our daughter Charlotte, we bought a house in Failsworth only to discover that my neighbour was a police inspector based in Oldham.

With all the moving we had done, I found myself struggling financially, so I began looking for a business that might earn me a bit of regular income. I tried to buy a lap-dancing club in Droylsden. They were very popular with businessmen at the time, and if a club was in the right spot it could earn very good money. After viewing the premises, I decided it wasn't for me, as it turned out to be much smaller than I had imagined. As I stepped out of the front door and onto the pavement, I noticed a 'For Sale' sign on a gymnasium across the street. I walked over, looked in and the following week I made an offer of £80,000 for it. The gym had huge potential, as it had two very large rooms, a bar and a seating area up on the roof; it was ideal for putting on boxing shows. My offer was accepted and I set to work refurbishing the place.

Shortly afterwards, I was offered £20,000 to fight against a Moroccan on Cape Verde, a group of islands off the west coast of Africa. I needed the money to refurbish the club, so I accepted the challenge. I won the fight quite easily and later that night I was introduced to a 32-year-old middleweight kickboxer who was extremely fit. His name was Eugenio Monteiro, but I called him Monty for short. Monty told me that he was sick of prizefighting and had dreamed of going to England to box professionally for a long time. I had watched Monty fight that night and knew instinctively that he had potential, so I suggested he come to England and I would train him. Monty claimed that he had personal matters to sort out before he could do so. I told him that the offer was genuine and left thinking that I would never hear from him again. A month later, Monty walked into my gym in Droylsden.

To be honest, I couldn't believe it really was him when he called out my name. Myself and an ex-boxer named Mel Kirk applied for Monty's boxing licence. Considering he wasn't resident in the UK and had never fought here, it was a surprise that he was granted one. His first fight was at the Marriott Hotel in Seaburn, in the north-east of England. Ricky Hatton was the guest speaker at the show that night. Nobody gave Monty a chance against his opponent, a lad from Gateshead named Danny Moir.

Mel, Monty and I were in the dressing-room when we were informed by officials that our bout was going to start in ten minutes. All we had to do was put Monty's gloves on, but before we could do so he took a plastic Tupperware container from his bag and opened it. The room was instantly engulfed in the strongest aroma I have ever smelt in my life. The smell was emanating from dry coffee powder, which Monty began spooning into his mouth. He didn't stop until half of the coffee had gone and then he washed it down with two cans of Red Bull. Mel and I looked at each other and couldn't help but laugh. We put on Monty's gloves and took him out to the ring. As soon as the bell rang to signal the beginning of the fight, Monty began smashing his opponent back and forth across the ring. The massive caffeine rush his body had been subjected to was clearly paying dividends.

The bout was scheduled over six rounds and Monty won on points. Before I was prepared to invest my money in a boxer, I wanted to know that he could fight. What I witnessed that night in Seaburn told me that Monty most definitely could fight, but I needed further assurances.

I rang Frank Warren, who is one of Britain's most famous boxing promoters, and managed to arrange a fight between Monty and Thomas McDonagh for the WBU light middleweight championship of the world at the MEN Arena. I was so confident that Monty was going to win, I bet £10,000 on him.

However, for the first seven rounds Monty looked as if he didn't want to fight. If you watch a recording of the fight on YouTube, you will see me grab Monty at the end of the seventh round, throw him in the corner and slap him hard across the face.

'Fucking fight him! What are you doing, Monty? Fucking fight him!' I screamed.

'I am not a dog,' Monty replied.

'I know you're not – dogs fight. Now get out there and fight,' I said.

Monty came out in the eighth round a different boxer; he won that round and every one thereafter. Sadly, it wasn't enough and he lost the bout on points.

After the fight, we went back to my club, where a celebration party had been arranged. I cannot celebrate defeat, so I went up onto the roof to smoke. Down below, I heard a commotion outside a bar in Craven Street. I could see several lads fighting, some of whom I recognised as Travellers. Moments later, the men began to run, leaving one of their opponents lying motionless on the pavement. Within minutes, the street was swarming with police and the body on the pavement had been covered with a sheet.

I didn't have a licence for the club, so I went downstairs, explained to people that the police were outside in numbers and told them that they would have to leave immediately. The police had no intention of coming into the club, but people celebrating a defeat was too much for me to handle. A defeat to me felt like a death in the family, and I just couldn't face being around anybody at such a time.

Within eight weeks, I had arranged for Monty to fight a Londoner named Gilbert 'The Hurricane' Eastman at the Derby Storm Arena. Eastman had recently won the BBBC Southern Area light middleweight title and was considered to be a tricky, hard-punching opponent.

The fight took place the night before my birthday. Monty arrived late, with another lad named Paulino Silva. I was fuming because I thought Monty wasn't taking the fight seriously and he was fuming because he thought I was being disrespectful to him in front of his friend. As I bandaged his hands in preparation for the fight, we were screaming in each other's faces. I was calling him a lazy bastard and he was calling me a control freak. Everybody else in the dressing-room looked sheepishly on, convinced we were going to start exchanging blows. We were still at each other's throats when we climbed into the ring.

Just before the bell rang, I grabbed Monty's head with both of my hands and said, 'Listen, whatever has been said, let's put it behind us. Go out there and take your anger out on your opponent.' Monty didn't answer, but he fought magnificently that night and won the bout on points. When the final bell rang, he walked over to me, kissed me on the forehead and said, 'Happy birthday, boss. That victory was for you.'

Eight weeks after the Eastman fight, Monty was booked to fight an Iranian named Mehrdud Takaloo at Wembley Arena in London. At the time, Takaloo was the reigning World Boxing Union light middleweight champion, but the fight against Monty was not going to be for the title.

The weigh-in was at the world-famous Peacock Gym in Canning Town. When Monty and I bowled into the gym, I began shouting at Takaloo, 'Look at the fucking state of you! My man is going to smash you! You aren't fit to be in the same ring!' Takaloo didn't respond. He just looked down and did his best to ignore me, but I knew he was rattled, so I continued taunting him.

On the night of the fight, I told Monty that he had to rush out from his corner as soon as the bell had been rung and smash Takaloo as hard as he could in the face. 'I promise you that he will go down. It doesn't even have to be a knockout punch, but he will go down,' I said. As soon as the bell rang, Monty did as I had asked and Takaloo dropped like he had been shot to the canvas. He managed to beat the count, but then he spent the rest of the fight running from Monty.

After the Takaloo victory, I decided to put on a boxing show at the Midland Hotel in Manchester. During my boxing career, I had fought half a dozen times at the Anglo-American Sporting Club, which put on shows at the Piccadilly Hotel in Manchester. I loved the atmosphere of those nights. Everything was so American: beautiful girls serving at the tables and announcing the rounds, immaculately dressed customers, great entertainment and, of course, quality food for the diners. It was like being back in New York for me. When Nat Basso had died, I had made it my business to find out who had the rights to the Anglo-American Sporting Club. I discovered that when Nat had retired from promoting in the 1980s he had passed the ownership of the AASC to a very good friend of mine named Pat Brogan. He had put on a couple of shows but they had not been successful. Promoter Jack Trickett then decided that he would try to reinvent the AASC. He called it the 400 Club and staged several shows at the Midland Hotel in Manchester, but these too failed to attract large audiences.

I then bought the rights off promoter Micky Duff for £30,000 and relaunched the AASC. I didn't have a boxing promoter's licence and so I went into partnership with a guy named Wally Dixon to put on the first show. The agreement was that Dixon would use his licence so that we could put on the shows; he would also do the accounting and I would handle everything else.

The boxing shows that I staged at the Midland Hotel in Manchester were extremely enjoyable events but equally stressful to arrange. How I never suffered a heart attack in the lead-up to one of those numerous shows I will never know. The hotel provided a conference room and a large basement room in addition to the main hall. I used to erect partitions in the basement so each boxer had a makeshift changing-room. In the conference room, I would provide a buffet, with tea, coffee and cold drinks for the fighters and their teams. Throughout the day, I would be running up and down the stairs screaming into my phone in an effort to ensure the lighting rig was being put up, the sound system was in order, the act providing the entertainment was en route and the boxing ring was being erected.

On one occasion, I instinctively knew that something was not quite right, but I was unable to pinpoint the problem. Walking up and down the stairs, I mentally ticked every potential problem off. Lighting rig, OK. Boxing ring, OK. Entertainers, OK. When I walked into the boxers' changing-rooms, I started to count the fighters. There were four bouts that night, so there should have been eight men, but I could only find seven. Brian Shaw, a fighter from Torquay, was nowhere to be seen.

'Hi, Brian, it's Wayne. Where are you, mate?' I said when he eventually answered his phone.

'I'm on the beach, Wayne, walking my dog. Why what's up?'

'The beach? The fucking beach? What beach?' I screamed.

'Torquay beach, Wayne. What's the matter with you?' he asked.

The blood had rushed to my head so quickly I felt fucking dizzy with rage. I shouted down the phone at Brian that he was supposed to be in Manchester fighting, but he only enraged me further by saying that he'd thought the bout was the following week.

I immediately rang an Egyptian guy called Iman who lived in Whalley Range, Manchester. To be honest, he couldn't fight, but he was game and had stood in at short notice for me on several occasions.

'Get your kitbag and make your way to the Midland Hotel as soon as possible, because you're fighting tonight,' I said when he answered his phone.

'No, Wayne, I can't. I'm taking my girlfriend out this evening,' he replied.

After listening to me rant for a few minutes, Iman eventually agreed to fight that night. He was battered by his far superior opponent and suffered a fractured jaw in the second round. By the time he was discharged from the hospital, his girlfriend had dumped him.

That night, every time I sped past the top table, which was reserved for VIPs, I could see Wally Dixon either roaring with laughter, eating food or drinking wine. To be honest, I was fucking fuming. At no stage did he offer to help me out, but then again he wasn't breaking our agreement, as his only concern was managing the finances.

To make matters worse, Monty turned up at the event and announced that he was signing a contract with a new manager.

'And who would that be?' I asked.

'Wally Dixon,' Monty replied.

I was so annoyed I couldn't speak. Every time I passed the top table thereafter, the sight of Dixon enjoying himself made me a little angrier. By the end of the night, I was ready to explode.

Two days later, I went to see Dixon and told him that I wanted £7,000, which was what I was owed from the show. Dixon produced scribbled notes on A4 pieces of paper and told me that the show hadn't made any money.

I didn't say anything. I just got into my car, drove home and picked up a typed set of accounts that I had kept. I then drove to a haulage yard where Dixon worked and walked into the reception area. I locked the door behind me and removed the key. Four lads were sitting nearby and one asked me what I was doing. 'I have locked the door so that nobody escapes. Do any of you have a problem with that?' I asked. The lads didn't reply. They simply bowed their heads and stared at the floor.

I walked upstairs and into Dixon's office. 'All right, mate? How's it going?' he said as I entered. I didn't answer. I just grabbed Dixon by the throat and dragged him across his desk towards me. After slapping him hard across the head, I dragged him along the floor to the accounts office. I kicked open the door and pulled Dixon in after me. '£7,000, please,' I said to the two girls who were busy typing. They looked at Dixon, who nodded as if in agreement with my request.

Moments later, as one of the girls began counting the money, Dixon said, 'You won't get away with this, Wayne.'

'Ring the police or ring a fucking gangster. I will wait here,' I replied.

Dixon remained silent, so I took the cash from the girl and walked back to my car. The ticket price was £700 per table and I had sold 40 tables. The show cost me £19,000 to put on, so I was owed at least £9,000 for the evening. Dixon, in my opinion, had therefore had a result.

I was genuinely upset that Monty had signed a contract with a new manager. We remain friends to this day and I genuinely love him dearly, but what he did was a huge mistake. I knew how to get the best out of Monty because he was a lot like me. My father had threatened and bullied me until the fire in my belly had been ignited, and I used the same tactics on Monty.

In fairness, his new management team did eventually get him a World Boxing Union middleweight title fight, against Anthony Farnell, which he won after knocking his opponent out in the tenth round.

However, he was immediately stripped of the title after failing a drugs test. Monty had nandrolone and an amphetamine in his bloodstream. His opponent was admitted to hospital after the fight and suffered 'complications', as a result of which he has never boxed again.

I felt that the AASC could be a success, but I knew that I would be unable to organise and run the shows by myself. I booked another show and then contacted a woman called Julie Perry, who ran a company called Revellers World Events. I told Julie that I needed help putting on the boxing shows and she arranged to meet me at my club. I watched from the roof bar as she arrived in a big Mercedes ML car. Julie oozed confidence and walked with such purpose and poise. I just knew that I was going to like her. We had a two-hour meeting, at the end of which it was agreed that she would handle the organisation and running of the shows. I was extremely pleased to have Julie on board; she is without doubt the best event organiser on the planet in my opinion. That is why she has been hired to organise events such as Wayne and Coleen Rooney's wedding and to assist Joan Collins with her promotional work.

One evening, Julie and I were invited to the opening of the prestigious 235 Casino in Manchester by a guy named Vince Miller. He had worked as master of ceremonies for me at the boxing shows and was a personal friend of legendary Manchester United manager Sir Alex Ferguson. When Julie and I arrived at the casino, Vince called me over to be introduced to Sir Alex.

'This is Wayne Barker, who runs the Anglo-American Sporting Club, Sir Alex. Wayne, this is Sir Alex Ferguson,' Vince said.

We shook hands and I said to Sir Alex, 'Very pleased to meet you. So what do you do?'

Looking slightly taken aback, Sir Alex replied, 'I manage a football club.'

'Really, what football club would that be?' I asked.

'Manchester United,' Sir Alex replied.

'Oh, right, I've heard of those,' I said, before making my excuses and heading across the room.

Everybody who attended the opening of the casino was given a few free chips to play during the evening. An hour or so later, I was sitting at a roulette table when Sir Alex walked over and sat down. For several moments, he didn't look at me, but then eventually our eyes met and he began to smile. As everybody knows, smiles are infectious, and so I too smiled and began to laugh. Sir Alex shook his head and said, 'You certainly had me there for a while.'

Because I had effectively sacked Wally Dixon, I no longer had a partner with a boxing promoter's licence. I therefore teamed up with a licence holder named Ian Robinson in order to satisfy the BBBC rules. The next boxing show was a huge success and everybody involved earned a good wage.

ROUND TWELVE

My Toughest Opponent

A SOUTH AFRICAN trainer in my gym named Sean Krull had been contacted by the local Youth Offending Team, who wanted to know if we could teach wayward children how to box. Because of my own childhood, it was something I felt strongly about and I wanted to help out in any way I could.

When the first intake arrived, Sean and I were pretty much left to our own devices, and we put the children, most of whom were in their early teens, through a pretty gruelling boot-camp-type experience. The vast majority rose to the challenges we presented, but one or two moaned endlessly, so I told them to sit out the sessions in the changing-rooms. This led to several formal letters of complaint being sent to me by the Probation Service, but I chose to ignore them. In my opinion, the probation staff needed more guidance than the kids in their care. Their world was full of fluffy clouds and fantasies; little they said made practical sense, to my mind.

One morning, I walked into the gym and caught a tall, lanky 17-year-old kid swinging on one of the punchbags, so I clouted him around the head with the flat of my hand. 'Get off the bag and give me 20 press-ups now,' I shouted.

'Mr Barker, what on earth are you doing?' a female voice shrieked from the back of the gym. The voice belonged to a card-carrying lesbian *Guardian* reader from the Probation Service, who gathered up the children and left.

The following morning, the 17-year-old, whose name was Arron Jones, walked into the gym and apologised to me.

'I'm sorry about yesterday. I really want to be a boxer,' he said.

'You couldn't box chocolates, son,' I replied, 'but if you're willing to do what you're told and work hard, I am willing to teach you.'

My gym didn't have amateur boxing club status and Arron was too young to turn professional, so I had to pay another trainer, Joe Pennington from Northside Amateur Boxing Club, to train him. Every time Joe arranged a fight for Arron, I would pay him £50.

Arron and I would regularly travel the country together taking on fighters on their home turf. Arron, or Prince Arron, as I renamed him, won his first four fights then suffered defeat against Anthony Small. The fight was stopped in the second round, but Arron had nothing to be ashamed of, because within six months his opponent became the Southern Area light middleweight title holder. Two fights later, Arron lost again, this time on points, but six months afterwards he claimed the vacant British Masters title after defeating Cello Renda at the Midland Hotel, Manchester. The hard work was paying off and I truly believed that Arron was going places in the boxing world.

One day, I received a call from a boxing promoter named Brian Peters, who offered me £25,000 for Arron to fight John 'The Derry Destroyer' Duddy at the National Stadium in Dublin. Duddy was a powerful puncher who had won every one of his twenty-one professional fights.

Despite Duddy's superior boxing record we accepted the fight. It was only nine days away, which didn't give us much time to study Duddy's previous fights and train, but I was still confident that Arron could put on a good show against him.

When the BBBC was made aware of the contest, they intervened and said they were unprepared to sanction the fight if it was to be over ten rounds. Despite the fact that Arron had fought ten rounds previously, they claimed that he wasn't experienced enough and could get hurt. They ruled therefore that it take place over eight rounds or not at all. I rang my counterpart in Ireland and confirmed that the fight was going ahead, but I can't recall if I remembered to tell him about the BBBC's concerns.

The day before the fight, Arron and I arrived in Dublin and booked into our hotel. We attended a press conference in the afternoon and that night I ensured Arron had an early night.

Ricky Hatton's brother Matthew was fighting on the same show that night and Ricky, who was in Dublin to support his brother, came into the dressing-room to wish us all good luck. Arron was looking sharp, throwing punches and shadow-boxing. He seemed totally focused. However, once we were in the ring and the home crowd began jeering and booing, Arron seemed to withdraw into himself.

The fight is still available to watch on YouTube. In round one, Arron initially kept Duddy at bay using his superior reach, but after being knocked down or slipping, his confidence vanished. In round two, Duddy knocked Arron down twice and the contest was stopped by the referee.

I was totally embarrassed by Arron's performance that night. People in the crowd were hissing and booing as we made our way back to the dressing-room. Several called

Arron a coward who couldn't fight. I have never had humiliation like that aimed at me. If you are losing, at least give it your best. Arron that night just didn't want to know.

I packed my belongings in a bag and as I stood up to walk out of the dressing-room Arron said, 'Wayne?'

'Save it. Just fucking save it,' I replied as I stormed out to a waiting car.

Back at the hotel, I was reluctant to go downstairs and join the after-fight party. I knew all my friends would be there and they would be asking what had gone wrong with my fighter. My problem was, whenever I had one of my boxers in the ring, I would be mentally and physically fighting the bout for them. I felt the joy of every victory and the pain of every loss. I could deal with either emotion, but I couldn't even consider humiliation or cowardice.

I went downstairs eventually and, as predicted, the embarrassing questions began to flow. After half a dozen Jack Daniels, I went up to Arron's room, banged on the door and ordered him downstairs to face what I had endured. Arron obliged but returned to his room after 15 minutes.

The following morning, the journey to the airport was made in silence. When Arron and I were driving back to Manchester, I broke my silence. 'I am so disappointed in you, Arron. You have thrown away the biggest chance in your boxing career. I have taught you to stand and fight for the past three years. I didn't teach you to lie on the canvas cowering. Watch the fight again. You constantly kept looking at me hoping I would throw the towel in. If you think you're taking a penny of the money we were paid for that farce, you're mistaken.' Arron didn't reply and didn't speak when I eventually dropped him off at his home.

Four weeks prior to the fight, I had renewed Arron's

232

contract, as I had not wanted to get caught out as I had been with Monty. His new contract had been drawn up for me by IPS Law, a company that represents many Premier League footballers, cricketers, rugby players and their agents. Arron's relatives had raised concerns about me doing this, because Arron still had a year to run on his old contract, but I had explained that I had invested a lot of time and money in Arron and I was simply protecting my investment.

When I refused to pay Arron for the Duddy fiasco, he reported me to the BBBC who summoned me to a hearing to explain my actions. I told them, as I had told Arron, that I pay my fighters to fight and not lie on the canvas cowering. The board tried telling me that I was in breach of my contract, so I gave them Arron's old contract, which still had a year to run, and told them they could keep it. 'I will mention that Arron has recently signed a fresh contract with me, which the BBBC has no involvement or jurisdiction in, and unless I get paid £20,000 Arron will never be able to get into a ring again,' I said, before walking out of the room. After three or four meetings with my lawyers, a relative of Arron paid me £20,000 and my relationship with Arron ended.

There are no hard feelings on my part, Arron knows how much my fighters have meant to me and he understands how let down I felt that night in Dublin. He has since said that he wasn't ready to fight Duddy, but on that point we have to disagree.

It had dawned on me that my quest to find a younger version of myself was never going to be fulfilled, and for the first time in my life I accepted that and walked away from the fight game. Not entirely, of course, because boxing was in my blood. I decided to put all my efforts into organising events with Julie, some of which would be boxing shows.

One Saturday night, we held a joint birthday party at my club for the managing director of Harvey Nichols and his daughter. The following night, former England, Manchester City and West Bromwich Albion player Gary Owen held his daughter's birthday party at my club. I had worked non-stop from the Friday afternoon, so by Sunday evening I was falling asleep on my feet. Foolishly, I thought a few Jack Daniels and Red Bulls would keep me awake, but they only resulted in me becoming extremely drunk. Julie was quite rightly annoyed and said so, which infuriated me, as I had worked so hard, and we began to have a heated argument.

The next thing I knew, the head doorman, who had been hired from a firm in Liverpool, tried to intervene. 'Hey, you big daft cunt, this is my club! Don't try telling me what to do unless you're prepared to fight me outside now!' I shouted. The doorman walked outside and when I took my jacket off and followed him he ran off up the street. I was absolutely raging by this time, so I went back into the club, switched on all the lights and told everybody to fuck off home.

Julie tried to calm me down and kept saying that it was only 11 p.m. and the party had been booked until 2 a.m. 'I don't care what fucking time it is! I want you and everybody else out now!' I shouted. Within 20 minutes, the club had emptied. Only my son Kane and I remained. 'I think I'd better drive you home, Dad,' he said.

I hadn't even sobered up, but I still knew that I had made a huge and embarrassing mistake. Julie Perry ended our professional relationship after that, and in fairness I cannot say I blame her. The reputation of my club also suffered because of my behaviour that night, and no further prestigious or corporate events were booked.

I tried to retain certain standards regarding clientele,

but the fewer the people who came to the club, the lower I had to drop those standards in order to keep the business afloat. Within three months, I was letting people in on the sole condition that they had enough money to spend on drink for the night. Inevitably, this resulted in the club attracting troublemakers, and fights were constantly breaking out on the dance floor and around the bars. It wasn't uncommon for me to be having five or six fights per night.

Ironically, the doorman I hired to help me keep troublemakers at bay in the club was none other than Brian 'Crazy Horse' Dolan, whom I had witnessed knocking down George King in the Long Bar in Piccadilly. Brian was an awesome street fighter who demanded respect from anybody he allowed into the club. When the troublemakers were under control, the club became popular again and I once more began taking bookings for wedding and birthday parties. As with all businesses, there were peaks and troughs, and during the tough times I was always trying to think of ways of bringing in more customers.

Because of the long hours I was spending at the club, my relationship with Sharon began to suffer. In time, it completely broke down. While working at the club one night, I noticed a beautiful girl sitting at a table and so I sent her over a complimentary bottle of champagne. To my surprise, she sent it back with a note attached saying, 'Thank you, but I don't know you.' I walked over to her, introduced myself and added, 'Now you know me, will you accept the champagne?' but she still refused. After a lot of persuasion, she eventually told me that her name was Claire Garnett and she lived alone in Audenshaw. To be honest, I was totally smitten with this young lady, and I invited her back to the club as my guest the following week.

After a couple of dates, I playfully patted her backside

one night and, to my horror, felt what I thought was a recording device in her knickers. I grabbed her, put her against a wall and shouted, 'You're a fucking copper! I knew this was too good to be true! You're taping me!' Claire looked horrified and terrified, burst out crying and demanded to be taken home. She continued to cry throughout the journey, so I assumed I had made an error of judgement.

'So what is it, then, if it's not a recording device?' I asked.

'As you can see my dress doesn't have pockets. I needed to bring my phone, so I put it in my tights, you idiot,' she replied.

I tried to apologise, but I was laughing so much the words wouldn't come out. Thankfully, Claire also saw the funny side of the incident and I was forgiven.

Within three months, we were an item and I had fallen head over heels in love with her. I don't know what it was, but something inside me changed after I met Claire. I think I may have matured. Instead of taking her to boxing matches, I found myself enjoying taking her to antique shops and tea rooms or for long walks in the country. Life for us both was simple but idyllic.

It was not long after this that I was diagnosed with cancer and underwent my first operation. I was eventually discharged from hospital with a possible death sentence hanging over me, my ravaged body weighing just 10½ stone.

When I got home, I jumped into my Land Rover Discovery and drove to the club. On my way there, a friend rang to ask how I was. 'I'm fine. In fact, I'm on my way into work,' I said. Clearly shocked by my nonchalant manner, he said that he would come into the club later to see me.

That night, a few friends arrived at the club to take me into town for dinner. I felt like I was attending my own wake, but I was determined not to show any negative emotion or anything that could be perceived as weakness whatsoever. I had left my vehicle at the club, so after dinner I began to walk home, which was approximately two miles away. The cancer made me feel extremely cold. It wasn't like the cold you feel in winter; this was a deep, numb sort of cold in the body. I therefore wrapped my body with two thick jumpers under an overcoat and put a woollen scarf around my neck before setting off. I don't mind admitting that every step I took felt like a marathon. Tears were soon running down my face in frustration after half a mile, but I was determined to prove to myself and others that cancer was not going to beat Wayne Barker.

My heart and mind were strong, but my body was extremely weak. After walking a mile, I sat on a garden wall and broke down before ringing Sharon, with whom I was still living. 'Can you come and give me a lift, please?' I asked. Sharon sounded extremely worried and, after lecturing me about being out at night after undergoing major surgery, she agreed to come and pick me up.

The next few weeks were extremely stressful. I was pumped with a cocktail of powerful drugs and underwent further surgery. I was told that a cancerous tumour in my colon had been removed and I should now undergo a course of chemotherapy. Most people have heard of chemotherapy, but few, I believe, are aware of what the treatment actually involves. I initially thought that I was going to be microwaved in some sort of adapted hospital machine, but that was not the case. Chemotherapy is a procedure where the patient is attached to a drip containing a poison that kills cancerous cells. Unfortunately, the treatment also kills cells in bone marrow, the digestive tract and hair follicles.

This results in decreased production of blood cells, inflammation of the lining of the digestive tract and hair loss. Many cancer patients put on a brave face and tell loved ones that chemotherapy isn't such a bad procedure, but it made me extremely ill, and quite frankly I hated and feared it in equal measure. Being bald already meant that it wasn't all bad news for me, however.

Some weeks after the chemotherapy, I was sent to the Highfield Hospital in Rochdale for a scan so the doctors could see what, if any, effect the treatment had had on my cancer. I could not believe it when I was told that the scan showed that the cancer had cleared. I cannot describe how I felt, but I certainly wasn't elated. A sixth sense told me that all was not well.

The following day, I attended an appointment at the Christie Hospital in Manchester. Sitting in the waiting room, I felt embarrassed about being ill. How strange is that for an emotion? I had never really been ill in my life before. I had always been fit. Yet here I was, dependent on others and unable even to hobble a mile. A couple in their 60s were sitting opposite me; both looked healthier than me. The man looked over and said, 'What's wrong with you, then?' I felt quite shocked that this total stranger had asked about my illness in such a casual manner. It was as if he was enquiring if I wanted a cup of tea. 'Cancer, mate,' I replied quietly.

'And what sort of cancer is that?' the man said. I didn't even know this guy's name, but something about his manner made me warm to him. Moments later, I found myself pouring my heart out to him. I explained everything about myself, my family and my illness in detail; things I had never told anybody else were described to him at length. The man was in a wheelchair and had been brought to the hospital from his home in Spain by his wife. He was a large man. His face had been disfigured by tumours and his feet were extremely swollen. When I looked into his eyes, I honestly saw death. At that moment, I felt extremely humbled and wanted to do anything I could for this man. I crouched down and repositioned his feet on the wheelchair supports before covering them with a blanket. I then made him a cup of hot chocolate in the nurses' kitchen.

It may sound like a ridiculous non-event, but that encounter changed my outlook on myself and my illness. Wayne Barker, the man who had believed he could take on anybody, was now as vulnerable as everybody else.

When I went in to see my consultant, he explained that although the scan had indicated the cancer was clear, I still only had a 10 per cent chance of surviving the next five years. 'What did you say, mate? I'll be dead in five years? I've just been told I am all clear. Are you on a wind-up?' I said as I rose from my seat. The consultant asked me to calm down and sit so that he could explain the situation.

'The CCT scan picks up tumours and cancerous cells,' he said, 'but there's no way it can pick up very small particles. Left untreated, these particles then grow into tumours and therefore you need to undergo a course of chemotherapy in the hope that any such particles can be destroyed.'

'How old are you?' I asked.

'I am 46 years old. Why do you ask?'

'At what age do you plan to retire?'

The consultant looked puzzled and asked what point I was trying to make.

'When you do retire, make sure you send me an invitation to your party, because this cancer isn't going to beat me. I want you to remember that,' I said, before walking out and slamming the door.

The medication I was put on made me extremely unwell

and uncomfortable. My feet and hands were like ice, and I generally felt tired and weak. My mind, on the other hand, was determined and unwilling to accept my fate. I began training, and because I couldn't face eating a standard-size meal I ate ten small meals per day. I began gaining weight and felt much stronger, so I pushed myself harder and began sparring.

During one session, I was allowing my opponent to hit me in the body in the deluded hope that it would strengthen my stomach muscles. After a dozen crushing blows, I felt my stomach pop and warm liquid began running down my legs. I pushed my sparring partner away, looked down and saw to my horror that the wound caused by my operation had burst open and I was bleeding quite heavily. I was rushed to hospital, where the wound was cleaned and stitched back together.

There was no way I could continue training as I had been, and this step back towards the grave, as I saw it, made me extremely angry and difficult to be around. When I saw people laughing and joking or couples embracing each other, I would think, 'Why haven't you got cancer? Why me?' At home, I began to vent my anger on Sharon. Initially, she tried to be understanding, but my anger became so intense that even she began to argue with me.

On 3 April 2010, I went to watch WBA world heavyweight title holder David Haye fight John Ruiz at the MEN Arena in Manchester. It was good to be able to forget my illness and lose myself in the occasion. For most of the evening, I was back thinking about the sport I loved, rather than checking the clock to see if it was time to pop more pills. Haye retained his title after putting his opponent down four times before knocking him out in the ninth round.

After leaving the arena, I was suddenly thrust back into reality. I was shivering with the cold, and morbid thoughts engulfed me. Self-pity turned to anger, and I began to focus on Claire and my children. What would they do if this disease killed me? The answer was obvious – mourn and carry on with their lives – but it wasn't an answer I wanted to acknowledge.

Wallowing in self-pity, I couldn't face going home, so I went back to my club. At quarter past one in the morning, I gave the keys to the doorman and asked him if he would lock up. I had never done that before, so he asked me if anything was wrong. 'I am unwell. It's no big deal. Put the takings in the safe and I'll see you in the morning,' I said.

I got into my Range Rover and arrived home just before 2 a.m. The house was in darkness, so I assumed that everybody was in bed. I made myself a cup of tea, switched on the fire and wrapped myself in a blanket, but I was still shivering. Alone in the darkness, I experienced a feeling that was totally alien to me: fear. I was absolutely convinced that I was dying. At 4 a.m., I shuffled up the stairs and woke Sharon. 'I think I'm dying. I can't get warm,' I said. Jumping out of bed, Sharon raced downstairs and returned with a thermometer. After taking my temperature, she looked at me in complete bewilderment and said, 'It's normal.'

The Christie Hospital had issued me with a 24-hour helpline number, which Sharon rang. After asking a series of questions, a consultant asked Sharon to put me on the phone. He explained that my core temperature was very low but this was not something I should be too concerned about as it was a side effect of the treatment I was undergoing. 'Wrap yourself up, get into bed and ask your wife to check your temperature every hour, and then give me a call in the morning,' the consultant advised.

Sharon helped me to take my shoes off before burying me beneath a pile of blankets in bed. Suddenly and without just cause, I turned on her. 'Leave me alone! Go away!' I shouted. Sharon left the room and I lay awake in the darkness until the first rays of sunlight signalled that dawn was breaking. It sounds pathetic and perhaps weak, but I began to wonder if I would ever see another daybreak. 'I can't fucking die here. I won't fucking die here,' I began saying out loud.

Sharon must have heard me because she came into the room and asked if I was OK. 'OK? OK? No, I am not OK. I am fucking dying!' I screamed. Sharon had obviously endured a lot while looking after me, and she too had reached breaking point. 'I can't live like this Wayne, you will have to go,' she said. I leapt out of bed and began shouting at her, 'I am beating this! You lot want me to die, so fuck you, I won't. This cancer won't kill me.' I then grabbed my clothing, ran downstairs, jumped into my car and drove off.

That night, I moved into Claire's home in Audenshaw where I remained for the next five months. Sharon thought that I had moved into the club, but I think she was trying to blot out the truth, as she had recently been commenting on the amount of time that I had been spending with Claire. I didn't have time to dwell on affairs of the heart. The way I saw it, keeping my heart beating was the only thing that mattered. If that failed, everything else would become meaningless, because I would be dead.

I went through four more courses of chemotherapy before I was given another appointment with the consultant who had told me that my scan was clear. When I arrived at the hospital, I underwent a scan and then I was told to go and see my consultant. As I sat in the waiting room, I hoped and prayed that the chemotherapy had destroyed any small particles of cancer left in my colon. Seconds felt like hours and hours felt like days as I waited for my name to be called. I had foolishly arrived early for my appointment in the hope that I would be seen sooner. Not knowing if I was cured or not was proving extremely difficult to deal with. Eventually, I was called and ushered into the consultant's room.

'I am sorry, Mr Barker. Not only has the cancer in your colon returned but we have also identified nodules on your lungs and in your liver,' the ashen-faced consultant said.

It honestly felt as if I had been shot by some sort of tranquiliser gun. I felt a hard, sharp pain. I slumped in my chair and for a second or two I was unable to focus. 'So what are you saying?' I asked.

The consultant explained that the cancer had spread and the only course of action available was to put me on a different course of chemotherapy. This was a ten-week course that gave me a whole new series of unpleasant side effects to deal with. I had to spend at least two hours in the toilet before I went to bed and the same length of time when I awoke. Thankfully, the ice-cold feeling in my hands and feet was no more.

Because of the drugs I was taking, I had to attend hospital on a regular basis. The corridor that linked the main reception area to the specialist cancer ward was 87 paces long. I know because I must have walked it no fewer than 200 times. Each time I did walk it, I was expecting further bad news, so I would try to avert my thoughts by counting my footsteps or the cracks in the walls.

As I made my way along the corridor one day, a sign that I had regularly seen suddenly stood out. 'Information Centre – Please Enter' it read. I don't know if it was curiosity or intuition, but I felt a genuine need to go in. When I did so, I was confronted by a wall of leaflets concerning skin cancer, breast cancer, brain cancer and any other type of cancer a human being could develop. I picked up every leaflet relevant to me and returned home, where I started reading. I learned that I had initially had Stage 3 cancer, but I now had Stage 4, which is commonly known as secondary cancer. The cancer in my body, I learned, was almost certainly incurable; in other words, I was going to die.

I left home clutching the leaflet and returned to the hospital. I walked down the now all-too-familiar corridor and, without knocking, entered the consultant's room. Fortunately, he was alone. 'Why didn't you tell me I had secondary cancer?' I shouted. The consultant looked embarrassed and asked me to calm down. 'Fuck calming down! Why didn't you tell me?' I asked. The consultant explained that he didn't want to tell me because he feared that I might give up the fight. He said that he wanted to see if the cancer reacted to the treatment by stabilising or reducing before telling me anything. I was in no mood to talk, so I walked out without saying another word.

Telling my children that I might die of cancer was one of the hardest things I have ever done. Not living with the three children I had with Sharon made it somewhat easier breaking the news to them. They had their mother and a home. I gave them love and financial support, but they were not reliant on me for anything. After I'd left Sharon, they had begun to learn to live without me. Sharon is 40 years of age, attractive, and will probably meet another man and start a new life for her and our children. For those reasons, I have no fears or concerns for them if I do die of this disease. My other children live with me, and telling them was extremely traumatic for all concerned.

When I was 17, my father took me to Stoke-on-Trent to visit my cousin, who had been diagnosed with cancer. When I had last seen my cousin, he had been a big, strapping lad with the strength of an ox. As my father ushered me into a private room at the hospital, I was confronted by the sight of a yellow, thin, almost skeletal man who was hooked up to various machines and barely able to breathe. There were two black holes where his eyes had once been. I was so shocked that I turned and walked out of the room. My father came after me and told me to return, but I refused. 'Why did you bring me here to see my cousin like that? He's a proud man. He wouldn't want me looking at him in that state,' I shouted. The incident really upset me and I vowed that if I ever ended up like that I would make sure I died alone.

Now that I knew that I could end up like that, I told my children that if a doctor ever told me that I had months to live, I was going to invite my loved ones and friends to a party, say my goodbyes and then move away to die alone. I explained that I didn't want my children to see and remember their father as an emaciated shadow of his former self. I hastened to add that I was born a fighter and the fact I was discussing my death by cancer did not mean that it was going to happen. I told them that cancer would not kill me, and to this day I firmly believe that to be true.

I began my fight anew by researching pioneering treatments. I read an article in a medical journal about a doctor named George Ladas who was a senior consultant at the Royal Brompton Hospital in London. In 2010, Dr Ladas had used the UK's first lung laser to operate on patients who had been diagnosed with terminal cancer. This, I decided, was a man I needed to meet. I booked an appointment to see Dr Ladas and, after examining me, he said that he could help. There was inevitably a 'but'. He could help with my lung cancer, he said, but he would be unable to assist me with my liver cancer. He explained that before he could treat my lung cancer the cancer in my liver would have to be removed. I told Dr Ladas to find me somebody who would be willing to operate on my liver, and within two days I had been referred to a consultant named Dr Mudan, who had a surgery in Harley Street.

When we met, he read my medical records and said that he might be able to help me. I would have to cease any chemotherapy courses that I was on, as he would need to operate almost immediately. The fees for the operations, the anaesthetist and ten days' stay in a private hospital were going to be more than I could afford, so I set about trying to earn or steal the money.

The price of scrap metal had gone through the roof in recent years because of the industrialisation of China. Copper was of a particularly high value, so I telephoned a few companies pretending that I was a potential purchaser. I finally found a company based in Birmingham that had nearly 25 tonnes of copper for sale, which they valued at approximately £250,000. I hinted at being interested, took the salesman's name and said I might call him back in a day or two. I rang back the following evening, haggled over the price and when I had secured a slight reduction I placed the order and asked for the copper to be delivered to a yard near Barnsley. I had friends in Brighouse whom I trusted, so I rang them and asked if they could find a yard for the copper to be delivered to in the Barnsley area. When they had found suitable premises, I faxed the address through to the Birmingham-based company and requested their bank details so that the money could be transferred when the copper arrived.

The following morning, two vehicles left Birmingham laden with copper, bound for Barnsley. I knew roughly what time they were due to reach Barnsley, so I sat opposite the yard in my car with my friends from Brighouse to await their arrival. The guy who owned the yard had no idea that I intended to steal the copper. As far as he was concerned, I had legitimately hired his premises as temporary storage space. The lorries arrived around lunchtime and I drove into the yard to oversee the unloading.

The first vehicle was backed into a warehouse and a crane immediately began to unload the copper. As the second vehicle began to reverse into the warehouse, it suddenly halted and the driver climbed out.

'What's the matter?' I asked.

'Is your boss about, mate? My boss wants payment transferred into his account before we unload any more copper,' the driver replied.

I explained that 'my boss' was in a meeting, but I would leave a message on his answering machine so that he could sort payment out when he was free.

The drivers sat in their vehicles and refused to unload anything else until they were given permission to do so by their employer. I knew they wouldn't sit there all night and that they would have no way of reloading the copper that had already been unloaded once the crane driver had gone home. I found out what time the yard closed and told the lorry drivers that my boss was due out of his meeting one hour later. 'I am not hanging about here all night, lads. The copper's safe. I'll come back in the morning when my boss has paid,' I said.

The drivers made frantic calls to their employer, who sensed all was not right and asked to speak to the yard owner. He was adamant that the copper would be kept under lock and key in the warehouse overnight. He had been paid for the use of his yard, and therefore as far as he was concerned there was nothing to worry about. The lorries were ordered to return to Birmingham and I drove off as if to head home.

As soon as the yard had closed, the two lads from

Brighouse picked up their friend, a wiry teenager with a long criminal record. The trio climbed onto the roof of the warehouse and lowered the teenager on a rope through a tiny air vent to the ground below. Once inside, he started up the crane and loaded the copper onto a vehicle which he then drove straight through the warehouse doors and yard gate. Because of the damage to the vehicle, I drove directly behind it, and the two lads from Brighouse drove in front in their own vehicle. We escorted the copper-laden vehicle to the yard of a man I knew in Leeds and I was paid in cash for it the following day. I gave the wiry teenager £100 and the lads from Brighouse £5,000, which left the amount needed for my treatment.

Now I had the money for the lung operation, I rang Dr Mudan and booked the earliest appointment possible. The following week, I had numerous blood tests, an MRI scan, a CCT scan and various other preliminary procedures. On 8 August 2010, I drove to London with my cousin and had dinner on Marylebone High Street. I had been warned that there was a possibility that I would not survive the operation, so it was an emotional farewell when he dropped me off at the hospital. That night, several of my friends in London came to see me. I wanted to remain positive, so I brushed aside talk of my illness and chatted instead about business. When they left around 9 p.m., I got into bed, but I found it hard to sleep.

Early the next morning, I was washed and prepared for the operation. After being wheeled into the anaesthetist's room, I was informed that the operation might take up to ten hours. If everything went well, I would spend five days in intensive care and then five days in my room, after which I would be discharged. I felt a sharp prick in my arm. Shortly afterwards, the anaesthetist's voice began to fade and then . . . nothing.

My first memory after that is of waking two days later. I am told that I had been awake prior to that but was heavily sedated. Pain isn't a word that describes how I felt. Agony does come close. Every move I made, however slight, required maximum effort. For some reason, my left leg wouldn't move at all. Through gritted teeth, I asked Dr Mudan if the operation had been successful. 'Very successful, Mr Barker. We have removed the cancerous cells in your liver, which equated to approximately 50 per cent. We did find additional tumours in your gall bladder and that has also been removed.' My liver, I was told, would repair itself over time and my gall bladder, which simply aids fat digestion, was not a vital organ.

My pain suddenly became bearable; I was winning the battle I had been warned might be unwinnable. The following morning, I somehow managed to get out of bed and get dressed. I then made my way to the reception area and asked if I could have a walking stick. The girl behind the desk walked away and returned with a crutch. 'That will do,' I said, before hobbling out of the hospital. I made my way to an Italian restaurant, where I sat at a table, ordered food I was unable to eat and savoured the fact that I was alive and free to do something normal.

After a couple of hours, I made my way back to the hospital. Two police cars were parked outside the main entrance and when I shuffled in a man began shouting, 'Mr Barker! He's here! He's here!' Apparently, the police had been called after a nurse had discovered that I was missing from my room. When a consultant came to see me, I thought I would be reprimanded, but he just laughed and said that I was the only person he knew of who had walked out of intensive care and into a restaurant.

The following morning, I thanked all of the staff and informed them that I was going home.

'But you need to recover, Mr Barker,' Dr Mudan said. 'I can do that at home,' I replied.

By the time I reached Manchester, I was in agony. I went straight to bed and remained there for nearly two months.

As I slowly recovered, things that had once been important in my life became less so and I concentrated more on its simple pleasures. Claire became my world, my everything. Being in her company made me feel alive. She made the cancer that raged in my body seem like little more than a headache. Of course, there was a downside to finding true love at such a late time in life. In my darker moments, the thought of having Claire snatched from me by death made it all the more painful to contemplate. The happier I felt, the bigger the comedown was when I was forced to face reality.

Because of this, Wayne Barker developed two personalities, one that I shared with the public and another that I reserved for myself. Outwardly, I spoke of a bright future with Claire. We were going to move to Knutsford in Cheshire, and we spent endless days viewing homes. We dined and drank in the local restaurants and bars and struck up several friendships with people from there. Inwardly, though, my dreams became nightmares. Realising what I could have had with Claire if I didn't have cancer broke my heart.

I purchased a home in Failsworth where we could both live and where my children could visit me without feeling as if they were taking sides. Sharon had initially accepted my relationship with Claire, but as I had become weaker the mood changed somewhat. I can understand why that might have been, which was why I thought a neutral home was the best option. James and Wayne came to live with me, and Claire spent at least six nights per week in the house, but things began changing rapidly. Since I have become bedridden, Sharon has kindly been looking after me on a daily basis. Claire no longer lives with me. This is not the way I want things to be, but for the first time in my life I am too weak to intervene.

As soon as I overcome this particular relapse in my health, I am going to get back into the gym and build up my fitness. I have done it before and I will do it again. As I keep telling people, this cancer will not kill me. I have too much to live for . . .

The Final Bell

ON 14 MAY 2012, Wayne Barker lost his fight against cancer. He was 52 years of age. I imagine that he was still calling for an enquiry into the result of his fight as he barged past St Peter at the pearly gates.

I was incredibly sad when I learned of Wayne's death. We had spoken in depth about many aspects of everyday life while writing this book over two long years, and I learned a lot about myself and life in general through him. My relationship with my own family has certainly benefited from my meeting him, because I realised what is really important in life as I watched his demise.

How do I end this book? How can I draw a line under a man who refused to stop living? The answer is I can't.

As I witnessed at Wayne's funeral, he has inspired many young men to achieve things they never thought possible. Arron, the disruptive boy he met via the Probation Service, who later became a world champion; Mickey, the single parent who described his victory against Frost as the proudest moment of his life; or Eugenio Monteiro, whom Wayne plucked from obscurity and turned into a world champion.

There are many more success stories in Wayne Barker's short life, and those he inspired will no doubt pass on all he taught them. The spirit of Wayne Barker therefore lives on, and for that his children should be grateful. I am extremely proud to have known Wayne and when I think of him only one phrase comes to mind: 'He was some man for one man.'

Bernard O'Mahoney